TEACHER'S PET PUBLICATIONS

PUZZLE PACK
for
Cry, the Beloved Country
based on the book by
Alan Paton

Written by
William T. Collins

© 2005 Teacher's Pet Publications
All Rights Reserved

The materials in this packet are copyrighted
by Teacher's Pet Publications, Inc.

These pages may be duplicated by the purchaser
for use in the purchaser's own classroom.

Copying any of these materials and distributing them
for any other purpose is a violation of the copyright laws.

© 2005 Teacher's Pet Publications, Inc.
www.tpet.com

INTRODUCTION
If you already own the LitPlan for this title, this Puzzle Pack will refresh your Unit Resource Materials and Vocabulary Resource Materials sections plus give you additional materials you can substitute into the tests. If you do not already have a complete LitPlan, these pages will give you some supplemental materials to use with your own plan. There are two main groups of materials: one set for unit words (such as characters' names, symbols, places, etc.) and one set for vocabulary words associated with the book.

WORD LIST
There is a word list for both the unit words and the vocabulary words. These lists show you which words are being used in the materials and the clues or definitions being used for those words. You may want to give students a word list with clues/definitions to help them, or you may want students to only have a word list (without clues/definitions) if you want them to work a little harder. Both are available for duplication. The word lists can also be your "calling key" for the bingo games.

FILL IN THE BLANK AND MATCHING
There are 4 each of the fill in the blank and matching worksheets for both the unit and vocabulary words. These pages can be used either as extra worksheets for students or as objective parts of a unit test. They can be done individually if students need extra help or as a whole class activity to review the material covered.

MAGIC SQUARES
The magic squares not only reinforce the material covered but also work on reasoning and math skills. Many teachers have told us that their students really enjoy doing these!

WORD SEARCH PUZZLES
The word search words go in all directions, as indicated on your answer keys. Two of the word search puzzles have the clues listed rather than the words. This makes the puzzle a little more difficult, but it reinforces the material better. Two word search puzzles have words only for students who find the clue puzzles too difficult.

CROSSWORD PUZZLES
Both unit and vocabulary word sections have 4 crossword puzzles.

BINGO CARDS
There are 32 individual bingo cards for the unit words and 32 individual bingo cards for the vocabulary words. You can use your word list as a "call list," calling the words at random and marking them off of your list as you go, or you could use the flash cards by cutting them apart and drawing the words at random from a hat (or box or whatever). To make a better review, you might ask for the definition and spelling of each word as you call it out—or you could call out the definitions and have students tell you the words they need to look for on the puzzle.

JUGGLE LETTERS
The vocabulary juggle letter game is intended to help students learn the spellings of the words. One sheet has the definitions listed on it as an extra help for students who need it or to reinforce the definitions if you choose to do so.

FLASH CARDS
We've included a set of vocabulary flash cards you can duplicate, cut, and fold for your students. Some teachers make a few sets for general use by the class; others make a set for each student. Some teachers duplicate them for each student and have the students cut & fold their own. You can cut out just the words and put them in a hat, have each student pick out one word and write the definition and a sentence for that word. Students then swap words and papers, with the next student adding a sentence of his own under the last one. You can have students swap as many times as you like. Each time the student will read the sentences written prior to his own and then add a sentence. You can cut out the words and definitions separately and play "I Have; Who Has?" Each student in the room draws a word and definition. The first student says, "I have (the name of the word). Who has the definition?" The student with the definition reads it then says, "I have (the name of the vocabulary word she has). Who has the definition?" The round continues until all words and definitions have been given.

Cry The Beloved Country Word List

No.	Word	Clue/Definition
1.	ABSALOM	Stephen's son who has become a criminal
2.	APPLAUSE	There is no ____ in prison.
3.	BUS	The Natives were refusing to ride the ____ in protest of increased fares.
4.	CARMICHAEL	Absalom's attorney
5.	CLOTHES	Gertrude's new ____ symbolize putting on a new life.
6.	COUNTRY	Cry, the beloved ____, these things are not yet at an end.
7.	DUBULA	Tomlinson has the brains, John has the voice, but ____ has the heart.
8.	ENRICH	Fear impoverishes always, while sorrow may ____.
9.	FEARS	Stephen has many of these as his journey begins.
10.	FOOLS	Nothing is ever quiet except for ____.
11.	GERTRUDE	Stephen's sister; he finds her living in immorality
12.	GUILTY	Verdict for Absalom
13.	HANG	Absalom was sentenced to ____.
14.	HLABENI	Taxi driver
15.	JAIL	Place where Stephen meets his son
16.	JAMES	____ Jarvis, Arthur's father. He donates things.
17.	JARVIS	Arthur; the murdered champion of the Native cause
18.	JOHANNESBURG	City Stephen goes to find his sister
19.	JOHN	Stephen's brother, a politician
20.	KUMALO	Stephen's last name
21.	LAWYER	Father Vincent's gift for Absalom
22.	LIES	John ____ about his son's involvement with Absalom.
23.	LIGHTS	The ____...fall...on the grass and stones of a country that sleeps.
24.	LINCOLN	Arthur Jarvis read about this American president.
25.	LITHEBE	Stephen rented a room from her.
26.	MILK	Mr. Jarvis's first gift to the children
27.	MISSION	____ House
28.	MKIZE	Said Absalom had been stealing and was in bad company
29.	MOUNTAIN	Place of spiritual refreshment for Kumalo
30.	MSIMANGU	Reverend who sent for Stephen, telling him of his sister's illness
31.	NATIVES	John speaks in public for their cause.
32.	NDLELA	Says the police are looking for Absalom
33.	PATON	Author
34.	PETER	Name for Absalom's son
35.	PIMVILLE	Place Kumalo found a native girl Absalom had abandoned
36.	SHUT	Once such a thing is opened, it cannot be ____ again.
37.	STEPHEN	Pastor who goes to Johannesburg to find his sister (& brother & son)
38.	TICKET	A young man stole Stephen's money for his bus ____.
39.	TRAGEDY	The ____'s not that things are broken. The ____ is that they are not mended again.
40.	UMFUNDISI	Word for 'pastor' or 'reverend'
41.	VINCENT	Priest from England who found a free lawyer for Absalom
42.	ZULU	The boy tries to learn this language.

Cry The Beloved Country Fill In The Blanks 1

1. The Natives were refusing to ride the ____ in protest of increased fares.
2. There is no ____ in prison.
3. ____ House
4. Nothing is ever quiet except for ____.
5. John speaks in public for their cause.
6. Stephen's son who has become a criminal
7. The ____'s not that things are broken. The ____ is that they are not mended again.
8. Name for Absalom's son
9. Stephen rented a room from her.
10. John ____ about his son's involvement with Absalom.
11. Author
12. Stephen's sister; he finds her living in immorality
13. Once such a thing is opened, it cannot be ____ again.
14. Stephen has many of these as his journey begins.
15. Tomlinson has the brains, John has the voice, but ____ has the heart.
16. Says the police are looking for Absalom
17. Absalom's attorney
18. The ____...fall...on the grass and stones of a country that sleeps.
19. Priest from England who found a free lawyer for Absalom
20. Arthur; the murdered champion of the Native cause

Cry The Beloved Country Fill In The Blanks 1 Answer Key

BUS	1. The Natives were refusing to ride the ____ in protest of increased fares.
APPLAUSE	2. There is no ____ in prison.
MISSION	3. ____ House
FOOLS	4. Nothing is ever quiet except for ____.
NATIVES	5. John speaks in public for their cause.
ABSALOM	6. Stephen's son who has become a criminal
TRAGEDY	7. The ____'s not that things are broken. The ____ is that they are not mended again.
PETER	8. Name for Absalom's son
LITHEBE	9. Stephen rented a room from her.
LIES	10. John ____ about his son's involvement with Absalom.
PATON	11. Author
GERTRUDE	12. Stephen's sister; he finds her living in immorality
SHUT	13. Once such a thing is opened, it cannot be ____ again.
FEARS	14. Stephen has many of these as his journey begins.
DUBULA	15. Tomlinson has the brains, John has the voice, but ____ has the heart.
NDLELA	16. Says the police are looking for Absalom
CARMICHAEL	17. Absalom's attorney
LIGHTS	18. The ____...fall...on the grass and stones of a country that sleeps.
VINCENT	19. Priest from England who found a free lawyer for Absalom
JARVIS	20. Arthur; the murdered champion of the Native cause

Cry The Beloved Country Fill In The Blanks 2

_____

_____

_____

_____

_____

_____

_____

_____

_____

_____

_____

_____

_____

_____

_____

_____

_____

_____

_____

_____

1. Tomlinson has the brains, John has the voice, but ____ has the heart.
2. Arthur Jarvis read about this American president.
3. Stephen rented a room from her.
4. The Natives were refusing to ride the ____ in protest of increased fares.
5. Pastor who goes to Johannesburg to find his sister (& brother & son)
6. Priest from England who found a free lawyer for Absalom
7. ____ Jarvis, Arthur's father. He donates things.
8. City Stephen goes to find his sister
9. Cry, the beloved ____, these things are not yet at an end.
10. A young man stole Stephen's money for his bus ____.
11. Absalom was sentenced to ____.
12. Verdict for Absalom
13. Stephen's last name
14. There is no ____ in prison.
15. Stephen's son who has become a criminal
16. Nothing is ever quiet except for ____.
17. Fear impoverishes always, while sorrow may ____.
18. Taxi driver
19. Stephen's sister; he finds her living in immorality
20. Place Kumalo found a native girl Absalom had abandoned

Cry The Beloved Country Fill In The Blanks 2 Answer Key

DUBULA	1. Tomlinson has the brains, John has the voice, but ____ has the heart.
LINCOLN	2. Arthur Jarvis read about this American president.
LITHEBE	3. Stephen rented a room from her.
BUS	4. The Natives were refusing to ride the ____ in protest of increased fares.
STEPHEN	5. Pastor who goes to Johannesburg to find his sister (& brother & son)
VINCENT	6. Priest from England who found a free lawyer for Absalom
JAMES	7. ____ Jarvis, Arthur's father. He donates things.
JOHANNESBURG	8. City Stephen goes to find his sister
COUNTRY	9. Cry, the beloved ____, these things are not yet at an end.
TICKET	10. A young man stole Stephen's money for his bus ____.
HANG	11. Absalom was sentenced to ____.
GUILTY	12. Verdict for Absalom
KUMALO	13. Stephen's last name
APPLAUSE	14. There is no ____ in prison.
ABSALOM	15. Stephen's son who has become a criminal
FOOLS	16. Nothing is ever quiet except for ____.
ENRICH	17. Fear impoverishes always, while sorrow may ____.
HLABENI	18. Taxi driver
GERTRUDE	19. Stephen's sister; he finds her living in immorality
PIMVILLE	20. Place Kumalo found a native girl Absalom had abandoned

Cry The Beloved Country Fill In The Blanks 3

1. A young man stole Stephen's money for his bus ____.
2. Says the police are looking for Absalom
3. Mr. Jarvis's first gift to the children
4. The ____'s not that things are broken. The ____ is that they are not mended again.
5. Fear impoverishes always, while sorrow may ____.
6. The Natives were refusing to ride the ____ in protest of increased fares.
7. Father Vincent's gift for Absalom
8. The boy tries to learn this language.
9. John ____ about his son's involvement with Absalom.
10. Nothing is ever quiet except for ____.
11. The ____...fall...on the grass and stones of a country that sleeps.
12. Stephen's sister; he finds her living in immorality
13. Stephen's last name
14. Stephen's brother, a politician
15. Priest from England who found a free lawyer for Absalom
16. City Stephen goes to find his sister
17. Stephen's son who has become a criminal
18. There is no ____ in prison.
19. Name for Absalom's son
20. Cry, the beloved ____, these things are not yet at an end.

Cry The Beloved Country Fill In The Blanks 3 Answer Key

TICKET	1. A young man stole Stephen's money for his bus ____.
NDLELA	2. Says the police are looking for Absalom
MILK	3. Mr. Jarvis's first gift to the children
TRAGEDY	4. The ____'s not that things are broken. The ____ is that they are not mended again.
ENRICH	5. Fear impoverishes always, while sorrow may ____.
BUS	6. The Natives were refusing to ride the ____ in protest of increased fares.
LAWYER	7. Father Vincent's gift for Absalom
ZULU	8. The boy tries to learn this language.
LIES	9. John ____ about his son's involvement with Absalom.
FOOLS	10. Nothing is ever quiet except for ____.
LIGHTS	11. The ____...fall...on the grass and stones of a country that sleeps.
GERTRUDE	12. Stephen's sister; he finds her living in immorality
KUMALO	13. Stephen's last name
JOHN	14. Stephen's brother, a politician
VINCENT	15. Priest from England who found a free lawyer for Absalom
JOHANNESBURG	16. City Stephen goes to find his sister
ABSALOM	17. Stephen's son who has become a criminal
APPLAUSE	18. There is no ____ in prison.
PETER	19. Name for Absalom's son
COUNTRY	20. Cry, the beloved ____, these things are not yet at an end.

Cry The Beloved Country Fill In The Blanks 4

_____
_____
_____
_____
_____
_____
_____
_____
_____
_____
_____
_____
_____
_____
_____
_____
_____
_____
_____
_____

1. The _____'s not that things are broken. The _____ is that they are not mended again.
2. Absalom's attorney
3. Stephen's sister; he finds her living in immorality
4. Place Kumalo found a native girl Absalom had abandoned
5. Says the police are looking for Absalom
6. Arthur Jarvis read about this American president.
7. Absalom was sentenced to _____.
8. Stephen's last name
9. Father Vincent's gift for Absalom
10. _____ Jarvis, Arthur's father. He donates things.
11. City Stephen goes to find his sister
12. Gertrude's new _____ symbolize putting on a new life.
13. The boy tries to learn this language.
14. Stephen's brother, a politician
15. Nothing is ever quiet except for _____.
16. The Natives were refusing to ride the _____ in protest of increased fares.
17. _____ House
18. Stephen has many of these as his journey begins.
19. Pastor who goes to Johannesburg to find his sister (& brother & son)
20. John _____ about his son's involvement with Absalom.

Cry The Beloved Country Fill In The Blanks 4 Answer Key

TRAGEDY	1. The ____'s not that things are broken. The ____ is that they are not mended again.
CARMICHAEL	2. Absalom's attorney
GERTRUDE	3. Stephen's sister; he finds her living in immorality
PIMVILLE	4. Place Kumalo found a native girl Absalom had abandoned
NDLELA	5. Says the police are looking for Absalom
LINCOLN	6. Arthur Jarvis read about this American president.
HANG	7. Absalom was sentenced to ____.
KUMALO	8. Stephen's last name
LAWYER	9. Father Vincent's gift for Absalom
JAMES	10. ____ Jarvis, Arthur's father. He donates things.
JOHANNESBURG	11. City Stephen goes to find his sister
CLOTHES	12. Gertrude's new ____ symbolize putting on a new life.
ZULU	13. The boy tries to learn this language.
JOHN	14. Stephen's brother, a politician
FOOLS	15. Nothing is ever quiet except for ____.
BUS	16. The Natives were refusing to ride the ____ in protest of increased fares.
MISSION	17. ____ House
FEARS	18. Stephen has many of these as his journey begins.
STEPHEN	19. Pastor who goes to Johannesburg to find his sister (& brother & son)
LIES	20. John ____ about his son's involvement with Absalom.

Cry The Beloved Country Matching 1

___ 1. MSIMANGU
___ 2. TRAGEDY
___ 3. TICKET
___ 4. LIES
___ 5. LAWYER
___ 6. MOUNTAIN
___ 7. LIGHTS
___ 8. MKIZE
___ 9. JAMES
___ 10. JOHANNESBURG
___ 11. GERTRUDE
___ 12. ZULU
___ 13. CARMICHAEL
___ 14. SHUT
___ 15. UMFUNDISI
___ 16. GUILTY
___ 17. PIMVILLE
___ 18. ENRICH
___ 19. MILK
___ 20. LINCOLN
___ 21. BUS
___ 22. DUBULA
___ 23. FOOLS
___ 24. CLOTHES
___ 25. KUMALO

A. Place Kumalo found a native girl Absalom had abandoned
B. Stephen's last name
C. Mr. Jarvis's first gift to the children
D. Once such a thing is opened, it cannot be ____ again.
E. Verdict for Absalom
F. Place of spiritual refreshment for Kumalo
G. City Stephen goes to find his sister
H. Word for 'pastor' or 'reverend'
I. Nothing is ever quiet except for ____.
J. The boy tries to learn this language.
K. The ____...fall...on the grass and stones of a country that sleeps.
L. ____ Jarvis, Arthur's father. He donates things.
M. The Natives were refusing to ride the ____ in protest of increased fares.
N. The ____'s not that things are broken. The ____ is that they are not mended again.
O. Gertrude's new ____ symbolize putting on a new life.
P. Absalom's attorney
Q. A young man stole Stephen's money for his bus ____.
R. John ____ about his son's involvement with Absalom.
S. Fear impoverishes always, while sorrow may ____.
T. Tomlinson has the brains, John has the voice, but ____ has the heart.
U. Stephen's sister; he finds her living in immorality
V. Said Absalom had been stealing and was in bad company
W. Reverend who sent for Stephen, telling him of his sister's illness
X. Father Vincent's gift for Absalom
Y. Arthur Jarvis read about this American president.

Cry The Beloved Country Matching 1 Answer Key

W - 1. MSIMANGU	A. Place Kumalo found a native girl Absalom had abandoned
N - 2. TRAGEDY	B. Stephen's last name
Q - 3. TICKET	C. Mr. Jarvis's first gift to the children
R - 4. LIES	D. Once such a thing is opened, it cannot be ____ again.
X - 5. LAWYER	E. Verdict for Absalom
F - 6. MOUNTAIN	F. Place of spiritual refreshment for Kumalo
K - 7. LIGHTS	G. City Stephen goes to find his sister
V - 8. MKIZE	H. Word for 'pastor' or 'reverend'
L - 9. JAMES	I. Nothing is ever quiet except for ____.
G - 10. JOHANNESBURG	J. The boy tries to learn this language.
U - 11. GERTRUDE	K. The ____...fall...on the grass and stones of a country that sleeps.
J - 12. ZULU	L. ____ Jarvis, Arthur's father. He donates things.
P - 13. CARMICHAEL	M. The Natives were refusing to ride the ____ in protest of increased fares.
D - 14. SHUT	N. The ____'s not that things are broken. The ____ is that they are not mended again.
H - 15. UMFUNDISI	O. Gertrude's new ____ symbolize putting on a new life.
E - 16. GUILTY	P. Absalom's attorney
A - 17. PIMVILLE	Q. A young man stole Stephen's money for his bus ____.
S - 18. ENRICH	R. John ____ about his son's involvement with Absalom.
C - 19. MILK	S. Fear impoverishes always, while sorrow may ____.
Y - 20. LINCOLN	T. Tomlinson has the brains, John has the voice, but ____ has the heart.
M - 21. BUS	U. Stephen's sister; he finds her living in immorality
T - 22. DUBULA	V. Said Absalom had been stealing and was in bad company
I - 23. FOOLS	W. Reverend who sent for Stephen, telling him of his sister's illness
O - 24. CLOTHES	X. Father Vincent's gift for Absalom
B - 25. KUMALO	Y. Arthur Jarvis read about this American president.

Cry The Beloved Country Matching 2

___ 1. MOUNTAIN
___ 2. LITHEBE
___ 3. ABSALOM
___ 4. BUS
___ 5. PATON
___ 6. MKIZE
___ 7. FEARS
___ 8. FOOLS
___ 9. ENRICH
___ 10. VINCENT
___ 11. CLOTHES
___ 12. UMFUNDISI
___ 13. MISSION
___ 14. SHUT
___ 15. JOHANNESBURG
___ 16. MSIMANGU
___ 17. JARVIS
___ 18. CARMICHAEL
___ 19. APPLAUSE
___ 20. STEPHEN
___ 21. TRAGEDY
___ 22. NDLELA
___ 23. JAMES
___ 24. LAWYER
___ 25. LIGHTS

A. Stephen's son who has become a criminal
B. Place of spiritual refreshment for Kumalo
C. Author
D. Word for 'pastor' or 'reverend'
E. City Stephen goes to find his sister
F. There is no ____ in prison.
G. The Natives were refusing to ride the ____ in protest of increased fares.
H. Nothing is ever quiet except for ____.
I. Absalom's attorney
J. Says the police are looking for Absalom
K. Once such a thing is opened, it cannot be ____ again.
L. ____ Jarvis, Arthur's father. He donates things.
M. Said Absalom had been stealing and was in bad company
N. The ____...fall...on the grass and stones of a country that sleeps.
O. Stephen rented a room from her.
P. ____ House
Q. Arthur; the murdered champion of the Native cause
R. Fear impoverishes always, while sorrow may ____.
S. Gertrude's new ____ symbolize putting on a new life.
T. Pastor who goes to Johannesburg to find his sister (& brother & son)
U. Father Vincent's gift for Absalom
V. The ____'s not that things are broken. The ____ is that they are not mended again.
W. Stephen has many of these as his journey begins.
X. Reverend who sent for Stephen, telling him of his sister's illness
Y. Priest from England who found a free lawyer for Absalom

Cry The Beloved Country Matching 2 Answer Key

B - 1. MOUNTAIN	A.	Stephen's son who has become a criminal
O - 2. LITHEBE	B.	Place of spiritual refreshment for Kumalo
A - 3. ABSALOM	C.	Author
G - 4. BUS	D.	Word for 'pastor' or 'reverend'
C - 5. PATON	E.	City Stephen goes to find his sister
M - 6. MKIZE	F.	There is no ____ in prison.
W - 7. FEARS	G.	The Natives were refusing to ride the ____ in protest of increased fares.
H - 8. FOOLS	H.	Nothing is ever quiet except for ____.
R - 9. ENRICH	I.	Absalom's attorney
Y - 10. VINCENT	J.	Says the police are looking for Absalom
S - 11. CLOTHES	K.	Once such a thing is opened, it cannot be ____ again.
D - 12. UMFUNDISI	L.	____ Jarvis, Arthur's father. He donates things.
P - 13. MISSION	M.	Said Absalom had been stealing and was in bad company
K - 14. SHUT	N.	The ____...fall...on the grass and stones of a country that sleeps.
E - 15. JOHANNESBURG	O.	Stephen rented a room from her.
X - 16. MSIMANGU	P.	____ House
Q - 17. JARVIS	Q.	Arthur; the murdered champion of the Native cause
I - 18. CARMICHAEL	R.	Fear impoverishes always, while sorrow may ____.
F - 19. APPLAUSE	S.	Gertrude's new ____ symbolize putting on a new life.
T - 20. STEPHEN	T.	Pastor who goes to Johannesburg to find his sister (& brother & son)
V - 21. TRAGEDY	U.	Father Vincent's gift for Absalom
J - 22. NDLELA	V.	The ____'s not that things are broken. The ____ is that they are not mended again.
L - 23. JAMES	W.	Stephen has many of these as his journey begins.
U - 24. LAWYER	X.	Reverend who sent for Stephen, telling him of his sister's illness
N - 25. LIGHTS	Y.	Priest from England who found a free lawyer for Absalom

Cry The Beloved Country Matching 3

___ 1. NATIVES		A. Stephen has many of these as his journey begins.
___ 2. UMFUNDISI		B. Name for Absalom's son
___ 3. LAWYER		C. Taxi driver
___ 4. BUS			D. Mr. Jarvis's first gift to the children
___ 5. HANG		E. Father Vincent's gift for Absalom
___ 6. MISSION		F. ____ House
___ 7. MOUNTAIN		G. Once such a thing is opened, it cannot be ____ again.
___ 8. CARMICHAEL	H. The ____'s not that things are broken. The ____ is that they are not mended again.
___ 9. HLABENI		I. Priest from England who found a free lawyer for Absalom
___ 10. STEPHEN		J. Pastor who goes to Johannesburg to find his sister (& brother & son)
___ 11. JAIL		K. Arthur Jarvis read about this American president.
___ 12. MILK		L. Stephen's sister; he finds her living in immorality
___ 13. PETER		M. Place where Stephen meets his son
___ 14. FEARS		N. The Natives were refusing to ride the ____ in protest of increased fares.
___ 15. GERTRUDE		O. Absalom's attorney
___ 16. TRAGEDY		P. Place of spiritual refreshment for Kumalo
___ 17. VINCENT		Q. Absalom was sentenced to ____.
___ 18. LIES		R. John speaks in public for their cause.
___ 19. NDLELA		S. Author
___ 20. JAMES		T. John ____ about his son's involvement with Absalom.
___ 21. PATON		U. Tomlinson has the brains, John has the voice, but ____ has the heart.
___ 22. LINCOLN		V. ____ Jarvis, Arthur's father. He donates things.
___ 23. CLOTHES		W. Word for 'pastor' or 'reverend'
___ 24. SHUT		X. Says the police are looking for Absalom
___ 25. DUBULA		Y. Gertrude's new ____ symbolize putting on a new life.

Cry The Beloved Country Matching 3 Answer Key

R - 1. NATIVES		A.	Stephen has many of these as his journey begins.
W - 2. UMFUNDISI		B.	Name for Absalom's son
E - 3. LAWYER		C.	Taxi driver
N - 4. BUS		D.	Mr. Jarvis's first gift to the children
Q - 5. HANG		E.	Father Vincent's gift for Absalom
F - 6. MISSION		F.	____ House
P - 7. MOUNTAIN		G.	Once such a thing is opened, it cannot be ____ again.
O - 8. CARMICHAEL		H.	The ____'s not that things are broken. The ____ is that they are not mended again.
C - 9. HLABENI		I.	Priest from England who found a free lawyer for Absalom
J - 10. STEPHEN		J.	Pastor who goes to Johannesburg to find his sister (& brother & son)
M - 11. JAIL		K.	Arthur Jarvis read about this American president.
D - 12. MILK		L.	Stephen's sister; he finds her living in immorality
B - 13. PETER		M.	Place where Stephen meets his son
A - 14. FEARS		N.	The Natives were refusing to ride the ____ in protest of increased fares.
L - 15. GERTRUDE		O.	Absalom's attorney
H - 16. TRAGEDY		P.	Place of spiritual refreshment for Kumalo
I - 17. VINCENT		Q.	Absalom was sentenced to ____.
T - 18. LIES		R.	John speaks in public for their cause.
X - 19. NDLELA		S.	Author
V - 20. JAMES		T.	John ____ about his son's involvement with Absalom.
S - 21. PATON		U.	Tomlinson has the brains, John has the voice, but ____ has the heart.
K - 22. LINCOLN		V.	____ Jarvis, Arthur's father. He donates things.
Y - 23. CLOTHES		W.	Word for 'pastor' or 'reverend'
G - 24. SHUT		X.	Says the police are looking for Absalom
U - 25. DUBULA		Y.	Gertrude's new ____ symbolize putting on a new life.

Cry The Beloved Country Matching 4

___ 1. NATIVES
___ 2. PIMVILLE
___ 3. STEPHEN
___ 4. BUS
___ 5. LINCOLN
___ 6. JOHN
___ 7. TRAGEDY
___ 8. TICKET
___ 9. MISSION
___ 10. APPLAUSE
___ 11. HLABENI
___ 12. ZULU
___ 13. FEARS
___ 14. DUBULA
___ 15. MKIZE
___ 16. MSIMANGU
___ 17. JOHANNESBURG
___ 18. GUILTY
___ 19. NDLELA
___ 20. LIGHTS
___ 21. LIES
___ 22. COUNTRY
___ 23. JAMES
___ 24. FOOLS
___ 25. MOUNTAIN

A. Said Absalom had been stealing and was in bad company
B. Stephen has many of these as his journey begins.
C. Nothing is ever quiet except for ____.
D. John speaks in public for their cause.
E. John ____ about his son's involvement with Absalom.
F. City Stephen goes to find his sister
G. Tomlinson has the brains, John has the voice, but ____ has the heart.
H. Cry, the beloved ____, these things are not yet at an end.
I. The Natives were refusing to ride the ____ in protest of increased fares.
J. Verdict for Absalom
K. ____ House
L. Says the police are looking for Absalom
M. The ____...fall...on the grass and stones of a country that sleeps.
N. Place of spiritual refreshment for Kumalo
O. ____ Jarvis, Arthur's father. He donates things.
P. Pastor who goes to Johannesburg to find his sister (& brother & son)
Q. The boy tries to learn this language.
R. A young man stole Stephen's money for his bus ____.
S. Arthur Jarvis read about this American president.
T. Place Kumalo found a native girl Absalom had abandoned
U. There is no ____ in prison.
V. Stephen's brother, a politician
W. Reverend who sent for Stephen, telling him of his sister's illness
X. Taxi driver
Y. The ____'s not that things are broken. The ____ is that they are not mended again.

Cry The Beloved Country Matching 4 Answer Key

D - 1. NATIVES	A. Said Absalom had been stealing and was in bad company
T - 2. PIMVILLE	B. Stephen has many of these as his journey begins.
P - 3. STEPHEN	C. Nothing is ever quiet except for ____.
I - 4. BUS	D. John speaks in public for their cause.
S - 5. LINCOLN	E. John ____ about his son's involvement with Absalom.
V - 6. JOHN	F. City Stephen goes to find his sister
Y - 7. TRAGEDY	G. Tomlinson has the brains, John has the voice, but ____ has the heart.
R - 8. TICKET	H. Cry, the beloved ____, these things are not yet at an end.
K - 9. MISSION	I. The Natives were refusing to ride the ____ in protest of increased fares.
U -10. APPLAUSE	J. Verdict for Absalom
X -11. HLABENI	K. ____ House
Q -12. ZULU	L. Says the police are looking for Absalom
B -13. FEARS	M. The ____ ...fall...on the grass and stones of a country that sleeps.
G -14. DUBULA	N. Place of spiritual refreshment for Kumalo
A -15. MKIZE	O. ____ Jarvis, Arthur's father. He donates things.
W -16. MSIMANGU	P. Pastor who goes to Johannesburg to find his sister (& brother & son)
F -17. JOHANNESBURG	Q. The boy tries to learn this language.
J -18. GUILTY	R. A young man stole Stephen's money for his bus ____.
L -19. NDLELA	S. Arthur Jarvis read about this American president.
M -20. LIGHTS	T. Place Kumalo found a native girl Absalom had abandoned
E -21. LIES	U. There is no ____ in prison.
H -22. COUNTRY	V. Stephen's brother, a politician
O -23. JAMES	W. Reverend who sent for Stephen, telling him of his sister's illness
C -24. FOOLS	X. Taxi driver
N -25. MOUNTAIN	Y. The ____'s not that things are broken. The ____ is that they are not mended again.

Cry The Beloved Country Magic Squares 1

Match the definition with the vocabulary word. Put your answers in the magic squares below. When your answers are correct, all columns and rows will add to the same number.

A. LINCOLN
B. HANG
C. NDLELA
D. VINCENT
E. FEARS
F. ENRICH
G. FOOLS
H. SHUT
I. NATIVES
J. JOHANNESBURG
K. MKIZE
L. ABSALOM
M. HLABENI
N. TICKET
O. MOUNTAIN
P. MILK

1. Fear impoverishes always, while sorrow may ____.
2. John speaks in public for their cause.
3. Place of spiritual refreshment for Kumalo
4. Priest from England who found a free lawyer for Absalom
5. Taxi driver
6. Absalom was sentenced to ____.
7. Once such a thing is opened, it cannot be ____ again.
8. Said Absalom had been stealing and was in bad company
9. Says the police are looking for Absalom
10. Mr. Jarvis's first gift to the children
11. City Stephen goes to find his sister
12. Stephen has many of these as his journey begins.
13. Stephen's son who has become a criminal
14. Nothing is ever quiet except for ____.
15. Arthur Jarvis read about this American president.
16. A young man stole Stephen's money for his bus ____.

A=	B=	C=	D=
E=	F=	G=	H=
I=	J=	K=	L=
M=	N=	O=	P=

Cry The Beloved Country Magic Squares 1 Answer Key

Match the definition with the vocabulary word. Put your answers in the magic squares below. When your answers are correct, all columns and rows will add to the same number.

A. LINCOLN
B. HANG
C. NDLELA
D. VINCENT
E. FEARS
F. ENRICH
G. FOOLS
H. SHUT
I. NATIVES
J. JOHANNESBURG
K. MKIZE
L. ABSALOM
M. HLABENI
N. TICKET
O. MOUNTAIN
P. MILK

1. Fear impoverishes always, while sorrow may ____.
2. John speaks in public for their cause.
3. Place of spiritual refreshment for Kumalo
4. Priest from England who found a free lawyer for Absalom
5. Taxi driver
6. Absalom was sentenced to ____.
7. Once such a thing is opened, it cannot be ____ again.
8. Said Absalom had been stealing and was in bad company
9. Says the police are looking for Absalom
10. Mr. Jarvis's first gift to the children
11. City Stephen goes to find his sister
12. Stephen has many of these as his journey begins.
13. Stephen's son who has become a criminal
14. Nothing is ever quiet except for ____.
15. Arthur Jarvis read about this American president.
16. A young man stole Stephen's money for his bus ____.

A=15	B=6	C=9	D=4
E=12	F=1	G=14	H=7
I=2	J=11	K=8	L=13
M=5	N=16	O=3	P=10

Cry The Beloved Country Magic Squares 2

Match the definition with the vocabulary word. Put your answers in the magic squares below. When your answers are correct, all columns and rows will add to the same number.

A. DUBULA
B. MILK
C. STEPHEN
D. LIES
E. APPLAUSE
F. GERTRUDE
G. JARVIS
H. FOOLS
I. KUMALO
J. PETER
K. UMFUNDISI
L. JOHANNESBURG
M. MOUNTAIN
N. MISSION
O. ENRICH
P. FEARS

1. Tomlinson has the brains, John has the voice, but ____ has the heart.
2. ____ House
3. Name for Absalom's son
4. There is no ____ in prison.
5. Arthur; the murdered champion of the Native cause
6. City Stephen goes to find his sister
7. Stephen has many of these as his journey begins.
8. Pastor who goes to Johannesburg to find his sister (& brother & son)
9. Fear impoverishes always, while sorrow may ____.
10. John ____ about his son's involvement with Absalom.
11. Nothing is ever quiet except for ____.
12. Word for 'pastor' or 'reverend'
13. Stephen's last name
14. Stephen's sister; he finds her living in immorality
15. Mr. Jarvis's first gift to the children
16. Place of spiritual refreshment for Kumalo

A=	B=	C=	D=
E=	F=	G=	H=
I=	J=	K=	L=
M=	N=	O=	P=

Cry The Beloved Country Magic Squares 2 Answer Key

Match the definition with the vocabulary word. Put your answers in the magic squares below. When your answers are correct, all columns and rows will add to the same number.

A. DUBULA
B. MILK
C. STEPHEN
D. LIES
E. APPLAUSE
F. GERTRUDE
G. JARVIS
H. FOOLS
I. KUMALO
J. PETER
K. UMFUNDISI
L. JOHANNESBURG
M. MOUNTAIN
N. MISSION
O. ENRICH
P. FEARS

1. Tomlinson has the brains, John has the voice, but ____ has the heart.
2. ____ House
3. Name for Absalom's son
4. There is no ____ in prison.
5. Arthur; the murdered champion of the Native cause
6. City Stephen goes to find his sister
7. Stephen has many of these as his journey begins.
8. Pastor who goes to Johannesburg to find his sister (& brother & son)
9. Fear impoverishes always, while sorrow may ____.
10. John ____ about his son's involvement with Absalom.
11. Nothing is ever quiet except for ____.
12. Word for 'pastor' or 'reverend'
13. Stephen's last name
14. Stephen's sister; he finds her living in immorality
15. Mr. Jarvis's first gift to the children
16. Place of spiritual refreshment for Kumalo

A=1	B=15	C=8	D=10
E=4	F=14	G=5	H=11
I=13	J=3	K=12	L=6
M=16	N=2	O=9	P=7

Cry The Beloved Country Magic Squares 3

Match the definition with the vocabulary word. Put your answers in the magic squares below. When your answers are correct, all columns and rows will add to the same number.

A. JOHANNESBURG
B. FEARS
C. APPLAUSE
D. MILK
E. JAIL
F. DUBULA
G. MISSION
H. GUILTY
I. UMFUNDISI
J. PIMVILLE
K. MOUNTAIN
L. NDLELA
M. VINCENT
N. CLOTHES
O. BUS
P. CARMICHAEL

1. Verdict for Absalom
2. Priest from England who found a free lawyer for Absalom
3. Stephen has many of these as his journey begins.
4. Place of spiritual refreshment for Kumalo
5. Place Kumalo found a native girl Absalom had abandoned
6. There is no ____ in prison.
7. Absalom's attorney
8. Place where Stephen meets his son
9. The Natives were refusing to ride the ____ in protest of increased fares.
10. Tomlinson has the brains, John has the voice, but ____ has the heart.
11. Word for 'pastor' or 'reverend'
12. Mr. Jarvis's first gift to the children
13. City Stephen goes to find his sister
14. Says the police are looking for Absalom
15. ____ House
16. Gertrude's new ____ symbolize putting on a new life.

A=	B=	C=	D=
E=	F=	G=	H=
I=	J=	K=	L=
M=	N=	O=	P=

Cry The Beloved Country Magic Squares 3 Answer Key

Match the definition with the vocabulary word. Put your answers in the magic squares below. When your answers are correct, all columns and rows will add to the same number.

A. JOHANNESBURG
B. FEARS
C. APPLAUSE
D. MILK
E. JAIL
F. DUBULA
G. MISSION
H. GUILTY
I. UMFUNDISI
J. PIMVILLE
K. MOUNTAIN
L. NDLELA
M. VINCENT
N. CLOTHES
O. BUS
P. CARMICHAEL

1. Verdict for Absalom
2. Priest from England who found a free lawyer for Absalom
3. Stephen has many of these as his journey begins.
4. Place of spiritual refreshment for Kumalo
5. Place Kumalo found a native girl Absalom had abandoned
6. There is no ____ in prison.
7. Absalom's attorney
8. Place where Stephen meets his son
9. The Natives were refusing to ride the ____ in protest of increased fares.
10. Tomlinson has the brains, John has the voice, but ____ has the heart.
11. Word for 'pastor' or 'reverend'
12. Mr. Jarvis's first gift to the children
13. City Stephen goes to find his sister
14. Says the police are looking for Absalom
15. ____ House
16. Gertrude's new ____ symbolize putting on a new life.

A=13	B=3	C=6	D=12
A=13	B=3	C=6	D=12
E=8	F=10	G=15	H=1
I=11	J=5	K=4	L=14
M=2	N=16	O=9	P=7

Cry The Beloved Country Magic Squares 4

Match the definition with the vocabulary word. Put your answers in the magic squares below. When your answers are correct, all columns and rows will add to the same number.

A. GERTRUDE
B. COUNTRY
C. ENRICH
D. JARVIS
E. APPLAUSE
F. LAWYER
G. MISSION
H. HLABENI
I. JOHANNESBURG
J. SHUT
K. DUBULA
L. FEARS
M. PATON
N. LIES
O. MKIZE
P. UMFUNDISI

1. Said Absalom had been stealing and was in bad company
2. Once such a thing is opened, it cannot be ____ again.
3. Taxi driver
4. Stephen's sister; he finds her living in immorality
5. Arthur; the murdered champion of the Native cause
6. There is no ____ in prison.
7. Tomlinson has the brains, John has the voice, but ____ has the heart.
8. John ____ about his son's involvement with Absalom.
9. Father Vincent's gift for Absalom
10. Fear impoverishes always, while sorrow may ____.
11. Author
12. Stephen has many of these as his journey begins.
13. City Stephen goes to find his sister
14. Word for 'pastor' or 'reverend'
15. Cry, the beloved ____, these things are not yet at an end.
16. ____ House

A=	B=	C=	D=
E=	F=	G=	H=
I=	J=	K=	L=
M=	N=	O=	P=

Cry The Beloved Country Magic Squares 4 Answer Key

Match the definition with the vocabulary word. Put your answers in the magic squares below. When your answers are correct, all columns and rows will add to the same number.

A. GERTRUDE
B. COUNTRY
C. ENRICH
D. JARVIS
E. APPLAUSE
F. LAWYER
G. MISSION
H. HLABENI
I. JOHANNESBURG
J. SHUT
K. DUBULA
L. FEARS
M. PATON
N. LIES
O. MKIZE
P. UMFUNDISI

1. Said Absalom had been stealing and was in bad company
2. Once such a thing is opened, it cannot be ____ again.
3. Taxi driver
4. Stephen's sister; he finds her living in immorality
5. Arthur; the murdered champion of the Native cause
6. There is no ____ in prison.
7. Tomlinson has the brains, John has the voice, but ____ has the heart.
8. John ____ about his son's involvement with Absalom.
9. Father Vincent's gift for Absalom
10. Fear impoverishes always, while sorrow may ____.
11. Author
12. Stephen has many of these as his journey begins.
13. City Stephen goes to find his sister
14. Word for 'pastor' or 'reverend'
15. Cry, the beloved ____, these things are not yet at an end.
16. ____ House

A=4	B=15	C=10	D=5
E=6	F=9	G=16	H=3
I=13	J=2	K=7	L=12
M=11	N=8	O=1	P=14

Cry The Beloved Country Word Search 1

```
M H L C M S I M A N G U P M M J H N
S O G B A L V J K Q H C I B I A A H
T S U G D R J U F J V L M U S R N R
E J V N J A M E S E I L V S S V G S
P O F P T A M I W N N S I R I I M N
H H B O L A M A C H E S L E O S O B
E N F O O R I O P H B Z L T N T L K
N M H N E L L N T P A F E E A R A Y
S G Q Y G N S O C I L E J P J A S P
H P W M W E L N T S H A L X N G B C
Y A H K V C R V S I L R U F D E A Q
L B T I B G E T Y D C S X S L D B L
C Z T N T U N N R N C K B P E Y N J
R A U W Z I R E T U G B E G L I A J
N Y H L M L I C N F D G R T A V W G
Q H S V U T C N U M Y E Z I K M Q P
V F Z J T Y H I O U D U B U L A Y D
L I T H E B E V C N V L M I L K P W
```

A young man stole Stephen's money for his bus ____. (6)
Absalom was sentenced to ____. (4)
Absalom's attorney (10)
Arthur Jarvis read about this American president. (7)
Arthur; the murdered champion of the Native cause (6)
Author (5)
Cry, the beloved ____, these things are not yet at an end. (7)
Father Vincent's gift for Absalom (6)
Fear impoverishes always, while sorrow may ____. (6)
Gertrude's new ____ symbolize putting on a new life. (7)
John ____ about his son's involvement with Absalom. (4)
John speaks in public for their cause. (7)
Mr. Jarvis's first gift to the children (4)
Name for Absalom's son (5)
Nothing is ever quiet except for ____. (5)
Once such a thing is opened, it cannot be ____ again. (4)
Pastor who goes to Johannesburg to find his sister (& brother & son) (7)
Place Kumalo found a native girl Absalom had abandoned (8)
Place of spiritual refreshment for Kumalo (8)
Place where Stephen meets his son (4)
Priest from England who found a free lawyer for Absalom (7)
Reverend who sent for Stephen, telling him of his sister's illness (8)
Said Absalom had been stealing and was in bad company (5)
Says the police are looking for Absalom (6)
Stephen has many of these as his journey begins. (5)
Stephen rented a room from her. (7)
Stephen's brother, a politician (4)
Stephen's last name (6)
Stephen's sister; he finds her living in immorality (8)
Stephen's son who has become a criminal (7)
Taxi driver (7)
The Natives were refusing to ride the ____ in protest of increased fares. (3)
The ____'s not that things are broken. The ____ is that they are not mended again. (7)
The boy tries to learn this language. (4)
There is no ____ in prison. (8)
Tomlinson has the brains, John has the voice, but ____ has the heart. (6)
Verdict for Absalom (6)
Word for 'pastor' or 'reverend' (9)
____ House (7)
____ Jarvis, Arthur's father. He donates things. (5)

Cry The Beloved Country Word Search 1 Answer Key

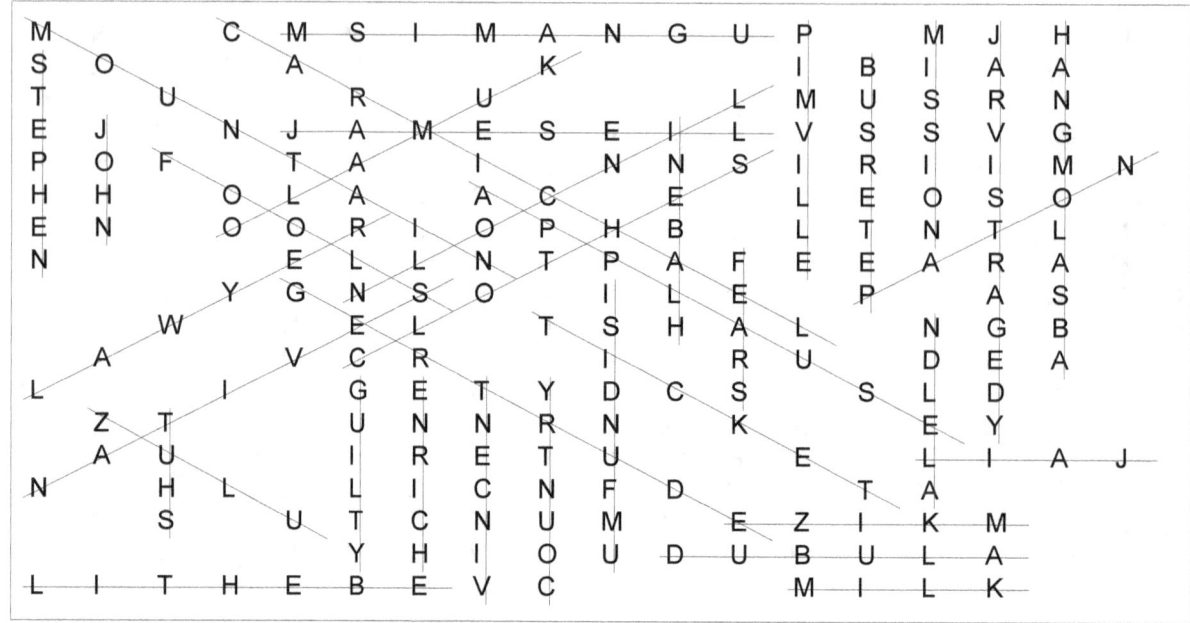

A young man stole Stephen's money for his bus ____. (6)
Absalom was sentenced to ____. (4)
Absalom's attorney (10)
Arthur Jarvis read about this American president. (7)
Arthur; the murdered champion of the Native cause (6)
Author (5)
Cry, the beloved ____, these things are not yet at an end. (7)
Father Vincent's gift for Absalom (6)
Fear impoverishes always, while sorrow may ____. (6)
Gertrude's new ____ symbolize putting on a new life. (7)
John ____ about his son's involvement with Absalom. (4)
John speaks in public for their cause. (7)
Mr. Jarvis's first gift to the children (4)
Name for Absalom's son (5)
Nothing is ever quiet except for ____. (5)
Once such a thing is opened, it cannot be ____ again. (4)
Pastor who goes to Johannesburg to find his sister (& brother & son) (7)
Place Kumalo found a native girl Absalom had abandoned (8)
Place of spiritual refreshment for Kumalo (8)
Place where Stephen meets his son (4)

Priest from England who found a free lawyer for Absalom (7)
Reverend who sent for Stephen, telling him of his sister's illness (8)
Said Absalom had been stealing and was in bad company (5)
Says the police are looking for Absalom (6)
Stephen has many of these as his journey begins. (5)
Stephen rented a room from her. (7)
Stephen's brother, a politician (4)
Stephen's last name (6)
Stephen's sister; he finds her living in immorality (8)
Stephen's son who has become a criminal (7)
Taxi driver (7)
The Natives were refusing to ride the ____ in protest of increased fares. (3)
The ____'s not that things are broken. The ____ is that they are not mended again. (7)
The boy tries to learn this language. (4)
There is no ____ in prison. (8)
Tomlinson has the brains, John has the voice, but ____ has the heart. (6)
Verdict for Absalom (6)
Word for 'pastor' or 'reverend' (9)
____ House (7)
____ Jarvis, Arthur's father. He donates things. (5)

Cry The Beloved Country Word Search 2

```
T I C K E T S T E P H E N F N M W K
M L D G E N R Y V L Q R L E L I T T
O P U L U L E A H C I M R A C S G B
U M B C R T H S G B C N G R Y S A S
N S U Y T N M J X E F N C S W I P K
T I L R R A J S D V D Q H O N O P N
A M A S E T A J V H X Y T D L N L Y
I A S X G I R D L J V F L P S N A P
N N P B X V V R I N G E B T E K U Z
P G A R U E I D T J L R H F K T S T
I U T U H S S T H A N G U L U Z E G
M T O P E L N C E L I H U Q M T Z R
V G N M O E I T B L A R J I A D I G
I P A O C R F D E S E B Z J L R K F
L J F N N G V R E Y L K E W O T M J
L Z I E L Y B I W W I N B N Z H Y H
E V J X M O L A S B A K K L I M N B
N S E H T O L C L W J C O U N T R Y
```

A young man stole Stephen's money for his bus ____. (6)
Absalom was sentenced to ____. (4)
Absalom's attorney (10)
Arthur Jarvis read about this American president. (7)
Arthur; the murdered champion of the Native cause (6)
Author (5)
Cry, the beloved ____, these things are not yet at an end. (7)
Father Vincent's gift for Absalom (6)
Fear impoverishes always, while sorrow may ____. (6)
Gertrude's new ____ symbolize putting on a new life. (7)
John ____ about his son's involvement with Absalom. (4)
John speaks in public for their cause. (7)
Mr. Jarvis's first gift to the children (4)
Name for Absalom's son (5)
Nothing is ever quiet except for ____. (5)
Once such a thing is opened, it cannot be ____ again. (4)
Pastor who goes to Johannesburg to find his sister (& brother & son) (7)
Place Kumalo found a native girl Absalom had abandoned (8)
Place of spiritual refreshment for Kumalo (8)
Place where Stephen meets his son (4)
Priest from England who found a free lawyer for Absalom (7)
Reverend who sent for Stephen, telling him of his sister's illness (8)
Said Absalom had been stealing and was in bad company (5)
Says the police are looking for Absalom (6)
Stephen has many of these as his journey begins. (5)
Stephen rented a room from her. (7)
Stephen's brother, a politician (4)
Stephen's last name (6)
Stephen's sister; he finds her living in immorality (8)
Stephen's son who has become a criminal (7)
Taxi driver (7)
The Natives were refusing to ride the ____ in protest of increased fares. (3)
The ____'s not that things are broken. The ____ is that they are not mended again. (7)
The boy tries to learn this language. (4)
The____...fall...on the grass and stones of a country that sleeps. (6)
There is no ____ in prison. (8)
Tomlinson has the brains, John has the voice, but ____ has the heart. (6)
Verdict for Absalom (6)
____ House (7)
____ Jarvis, Arthur's father. He donates things. (5)

Cry The Beloved Country Word Search 2 Answer Key

```
T I C K E T S T E P H E N F     M
M     D     D     R       L     E     I
O     U     U   L E A H C I M R A C S
U M   B     R       G       N R   O S   A
N S   U   T   N         E       C S   N   P
T I   L   R   A J       D           O   O P
A M   A   E   T A     L       L   P   S N L
I A       G   I R     I       E   S   E N A
N N P   B   V V     T       L   T   K   U
P G A   U E I     T     L     H U L Z   S
I U T U H S S T H A N G U L   Z   E
M   O   E L N C E   L   I       U   M   Z R
V   N M O E I     B   A R     I   A   I
I   A O C R       E S E B     J L   O T K
L J F N N         E   Y L     E     O   T M
L   I E               W   I       N   H   Y
E V       M O L A S B A     K L   M   N
S E H T O L C       J   C O U N T R Y
```

A young man stole Stephen's money for his bus ____. (6)
Absalom was sentenced to ____. (4)
Absalom's attorney (10)
Arthur Jarvis read about this American president. (7)
Arthur; the murdered champion of the Native cause (6)
Author (5)
Cry, the beloved ____, these things are not yet at an end. (7)
Father Vincent's gift for Absalom (6)
Fear impoverishes always, while sorrow may ____. (6)
Gertrude's new ____ symbolize putting on a new life. (7)
John ____ about his son's involvement with Absalom. (4)
John speaks in public for their cause. (7)
Mr. Jarvis's first gift to the children (4)
Name for Absalom's son (5)
Nothing is ever quiet except for ____. (5)
Once such a thing is opened, it cannot be ____ again. (4)
Pastor who goes to Johannesburg to find his sister (& brother & son) (7)
Place Kumalo found a native girl Absalom had abandoned (8)
Place of spiritual refreshment for Kumalo (8)
Place where Stephen meets his son (4)

Priest from England who found a free lawyer for Absalom (7)
Reverend who sent for Stephen, telling him of his sister's illness (8)
Said Absalom had been stealing and was in bad company (5)
Says the police are looking for Absalom (6)
Stephen has many of these as his journey begins. (5)
Stephen rented a room from her. (7)
Stephen's brother, a politician (4)
Stephen's last name (6)
Stephen's sister; he finds her living in immorality (8)
Stephen's son who has become a criminal (7)
Taxi driver (7)
The Natives were refusing to ride the ____ in protest of increased fares. (3)
The ____'s not that things are broken. The ____ is that they are not mended again. (7)
The boy tries to learn this language. (4)
The____...fall...on the grass and stones of a country that sleeps. (6)
There is no ____ in prison. (8)
Tomlinson has the brains, John has the voice, but ____ has the heart. (6)
Verdict for Absalom (6)
____ House (7)
____ Jarvis, Arthur's father. He donates things. (5)

Cry The Beloved Country Word Search 3

```
M T C L M T C J S Z P W K R X C J S K V
I I O I N O Y O K S V N P F W A K H G R
L C U T D J U H F G Q E W S M S F U E R
K K N H Q V I N C E N T N E H P E T S N
T E T E A H Q L T R A L S H L B E R J R
A T R B G N D O I A M R K T A P L A O D
L R Y E X S G C K Z I C S O B J L G H K
E I M J L T H N U G U N U L E A I E A S
L H E O E H B I M M L B C N I V D N Z
D P O S A G T L A D H M U F I L M Y N Q
N F P S H I Y T L I U G K R C I G E W
D V A L C L N G O H Y B O P E P P E S N
W D T M I U J B Z B R L U Z Y Q M R B C
J C O N M G Y M N G A Z T L W K I T U Z
N A N F R N W V M S E V I T A N S R R X
D M R P A R L B W K B M W L G S U G P
F N Z V C M S A C S N H H K K B I D X L
B C H T I I S I D N U F M U I Z O E J Q
T P F J E S U A L P P A B R V Z N V V D
X V R S C M L W Y Y B M M H R B E K L C
```

ABSALOM
APPLAUSE
BUS
CARMICHAEL
CLOTHES
COUNTRY
DUBULA
ENRICH
FEARS
FOOLS
GERTRUDE
GUILTY
HANG
HLABENI

JAIL
JAMES
JARVIS
JOHANNESBURG
JOHN
KUMALO
LAWYER
LIES
LIGHTS
LINCOLN
LITHEBE
MILK
MISSION
MKIZE

MOUNTAIN
MSIMANGU
NATIVES
NDLELA
PATON
PETER
PIMVILLE
SHUT
STEPHEN
TICKET
TRAGEDY
UMFUNDISI
VINCENT
ZULU

Cry The Beloved Country Word Search 3 Answer Key

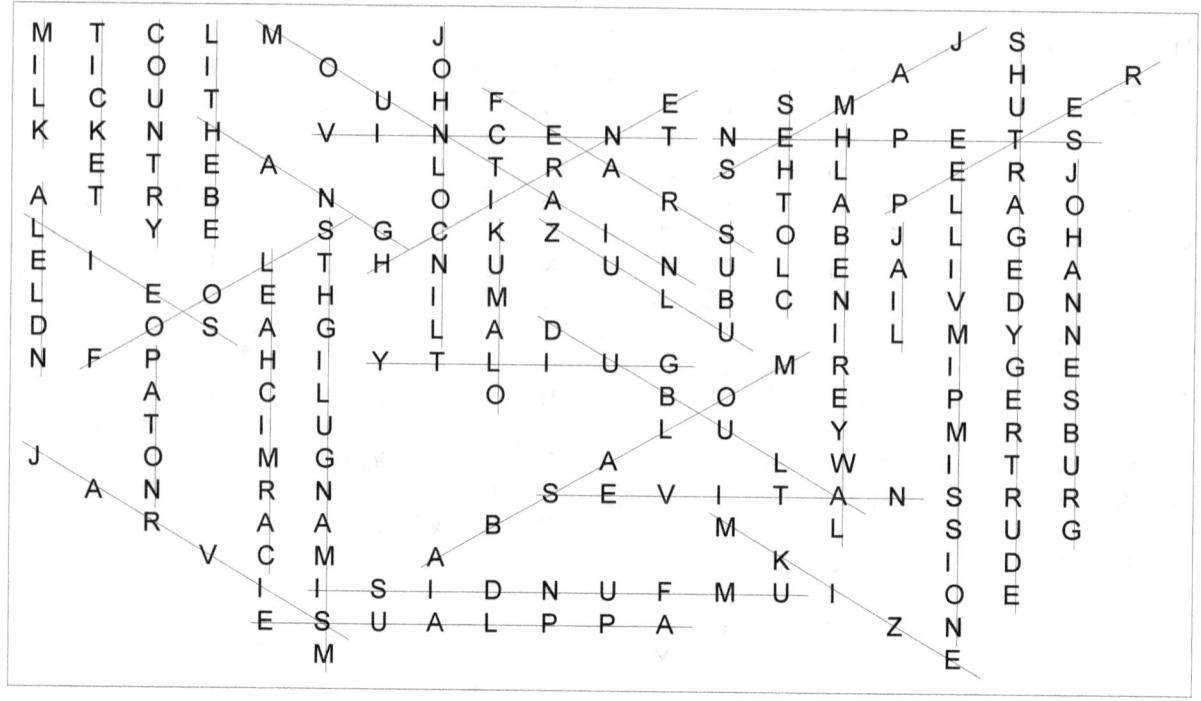

ABSALOM	JAIL	MOUNTAIN
APPLAUSE	JAMES	MSIMANGU
BUS	JARVIS	NATIVES
CARMICHAEL	JOHANNESBURG	NDLELA
CLOTHES	JOHN	PATON
COUNTRY	KUMALO	PETER
DUBULA	LAWYER	PIMVILLE
ENRICH	LIES	SHUT
FEARS	LIGHTS	STEPHEN
FOOLS	LINCOLN	TICKET
GERTRUDE	LITHEBE	TRAGEDY
GUILTY	MILK	UMFUNDISI
HANG	MISSION	VINCENT
HLABENI	MKIZE	ZULU

Cry The Beloved Country Word Search 4

```
P U G N A M I S M S D N H V J Z L I A J
E I N V M P R M R I O N A I J A U A M B M
T T M H P M P A K T L P N N M L W K S F
E Y R V K K E L A D M K G C E U Y I A N
R R K A I F S P A H Q Z H E S G E Z L T
K T F C G L G V C U S M G N N L R E O N
D N W Q X E L Q A X S B B T F V Z D M H
M U B C X Y D E R V S E N D L E L A F W
K O R X F K E Y M G T K X J B J L P B C
R C U N J T B X I N E D T J A S B M K W
V T Z N Z L E C C B P R T H L R P H J Y
H I T L T V H C H T H Q T H U S V W F H
L C Y V Q A T M A S E Z T R B X W I C T
A K S W S E I L E E N U M F U N D I S I
B E P S R S L N L H L W L V D R C G V
E T R G S S J S O T O K I S Y N E H U D
N Q W I L X S J V O C V G D E S F R I G
I B O O L A M U K L N M H S W H S P L Y
G N O X M G B Q J C I Y T X J U Z D T S
P F N A T I V E S P L Y S F B T X K Y Z
```

ABSALOM
APPLAUSE
BUS
CARMICHAEL
CLOTHES
COUNTRY
DUBULA
ENRICH
FEARS
FOOLS
GERTRUDE

GUILTY
HANG
HLABENI
JAIL
JAMES
JARVIS
JOHN
KUMALO
LAWYER
LIES
LIGHTS

LINCOLN
LITHEBE
MILK
MISSION
MKIZE
MOUNTAIN
MSIMANGU
NATIVES
NDLELA
PATON
PETER

PIMVILLE
SHUT
STEPHEN
TICKET
TRAGEDY
UMFUNDISI
VINCENT
ZULU

Cry The Beloved Country Word Search 4 Answer Key

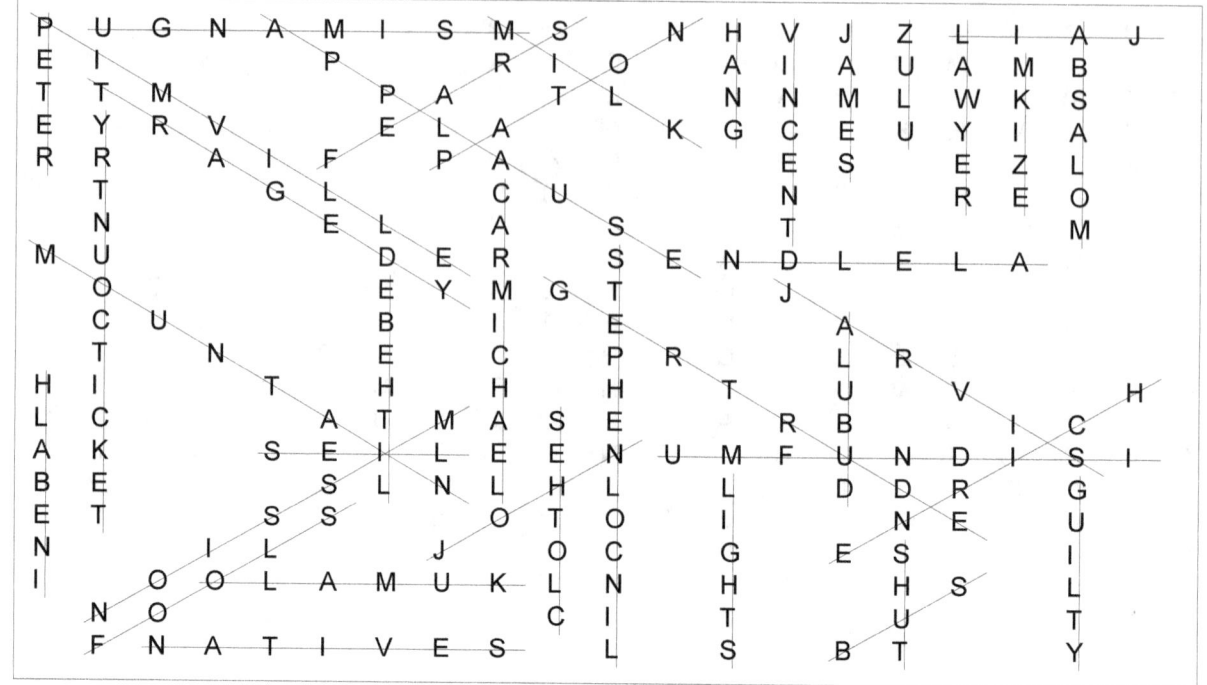

ABSALOM	GUILTY	LINCOLN	PIMVILLE
APPLAUSE	HANG	LITHEBE	SHUT
BUS	HLABENI	MILK	STEPHEN
CARMICHAEL	JAIL	MISSION	TICKET
CLOTHES	JAMES	MKIZE	TRAGEDY
COUNTRY	JARVIS	MOUNTAIN	UMFUNDISI
DUBULA	JOHN	MSIMANGU	VINCENT
ENRICH	KUMALO	NATIVES	ZULU
FEARS	LAWYER	NDLELA	
FOOLS	LIES	PATON	
GERTRUDE	LIGHTS	PETER	

Cry The Beloved Country Crossword 1

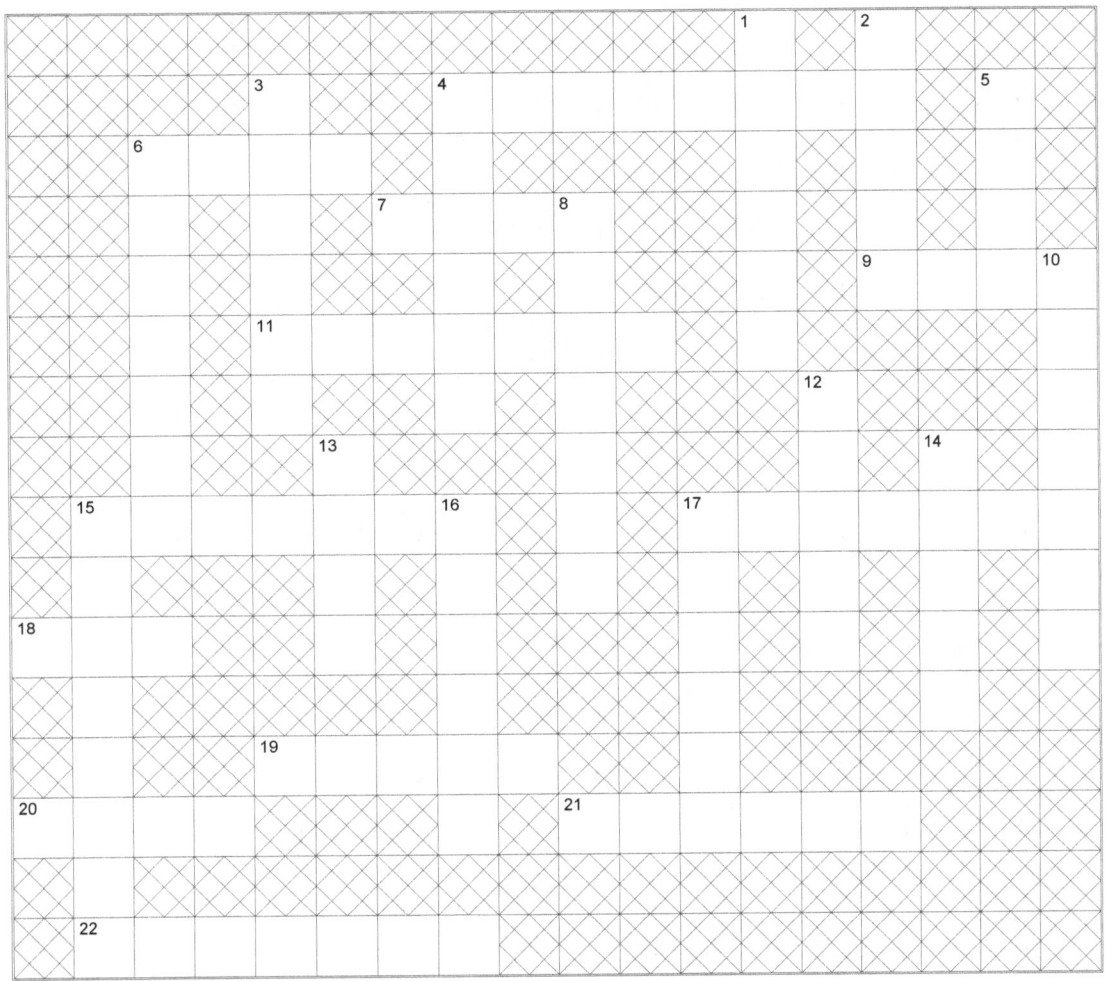

Across

4. Stephen's sister; he finds her living in immorality
6. Absalom was sentenced to ____.
7. John ____ about his son's involvement with Absalom.
9. Once such a thing is opened, it cannot be ____ again.
11. Gertrude's new ____ symbolize putting on a new life.
15. ____ House
17. Stephen rented a room from her.
18. The Natives were refusing to ride the ____ in protest of increased fares.
19. Nothing is ever quiet except for ____.
20. Place where Stephen meets his son
21. Arthur; the murdered champion of the Native cause
22. John speaks in public for their cause.

Down

1. Stephen's last name
2. Stephen has many of these as his journey begins.
3. Fear impoverishes always, while sorrow may ____.
4. Verdict for Absalom
5. The boy tries to learn this language.
6. Taxi driver
8. Pastor who goes to Johannesburg to find his sister (& brother & son)
10. The ____'s not that things are broken. The ____ is that they are not mended again.
12. Author
13. Mr. Jarvis's first gift to the children
14. Name for Absalom's son
15. Place of spiritual refreshment for Kumalo
16. Says the police are looking for Absalom
17. Father Vincent's gift for Absalom

Cry The Beloved Country Crossword 1 Answer Key

								1 K		2 F		
		3 E		4 G	E	R	T	R	U	D	E	5 Z
	6 H	A	N	G	U				M		A	U
	L	R		7 L	I	E	8 S		A		R	L
	A	I		L			T		L		9 S	H	U	10 T
	B	11 C	L	O	T	H	E	S	O			R
	E	H		Y			P			12 P		A
	N		13 M				H			A	14 P	G
15 M	I	S	S	I	O	16 N		E	17 L	I	T	H	E	B	E
	O		L		D		E		A		O	T	D
18 B	U	S		K		L			W		N	E	Y
	N					E			Y			R	
	T		19 F	O	O	L	S		E				
20 J	A	I	L			A		21 J	A	R	V	I	S
	I												
	22 N	A	T	I	V	E	S						

Across
4. Stephen's sister; he finds her living in immorality
6. Absalom was sentenced to ____.
7. John ____ about his son's involvement with Absalom.
9. Once such a thing is opened, it cannot be ____ again.
11. Gertrude's new ____ symbolize putting on a new life.
15. ____ House
17. Stephen rented a room from her.
18. The Natives were refusing to ride the ____ in protest of increased fares.
19. Nothing is ever quiet except for ____.
20. Place where Stephen meets his son
21. Arthur; the murdered champion of the Native cause
22. John speaks in public for their cause.

Down
1. Stephen's last name
2. Stephen has many of these as his journey begins.
3. Fear impoverishes always, while sorrow may ____.
4. Verdict for Absalom
5. The boy tries to learn this language.
6. Taxi driver
8. Pastor who goes to Johannesburg to find his sister (& brother & son)
10. The ____'s not that things are broken. The ____ is that they are not mended again.
12. Author
13. Mr. Jarvis's first gift to the children
14. Name for Absalom's son
15. Place of spiritual refreshment for Kumalo
16. Says the police are looking for Absalom
17. Father Vincent's gift for Absalom

Cry The Beloved Country Crossword 2

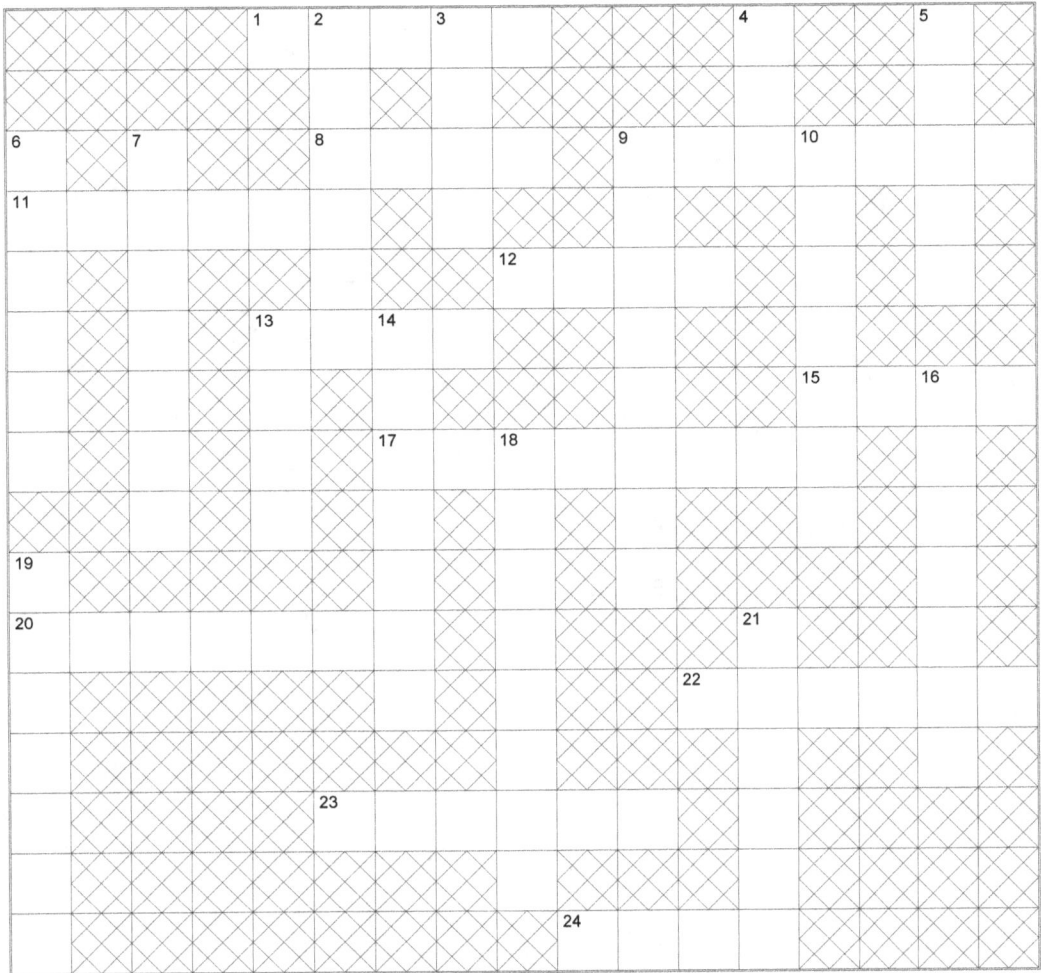

Across

1. Said Absalom had been stealing and was in bad company
8. Mr. Jarvis's first gift to the children
9. ____ House
11. Tomlinson has the brains, John has the voice, but ____ has the heart.
12. Once such a thing is opened, it cannot be ____ again.
13. Stephen's brother, a politician
15. Absalom was sentenced to ____.
17. There is no ____ in prison.
20. Arthur Jarvis read about this American president.
22. A young man stole Stephen's money for his bus ____.
23. Verdict for Absalom
24. John ____ about his son's involvement with Absalom.

Down

2. Stephen's last name
3. The boy tries to learn this language.
4. The Natives were refusing to ride the ____ in protest of increased fares.
5. Nothing is ever quiet except for ____.
6. Says the police are looking for Absalom
7. Stephen's son who has become a criminal
9. Place of spiritual refreshment for Kumalo
10. Pastor who goes to Johannesburg to find his sister (& brother & son)
13. Place where Stephen meets his son
14. Taxi driver
16. John speaks in public for their cause.
18. Place Kumalo found a native girl Absalom had abandoned
19. Gertrude's new ____ symbolize putting on a new life.
21. The____...fall...on the grass and stones of a country that sleeps.

Cry The Beloved Country Crossword 2 Answer Key

		1 M	2 K	I	3 Z	E			4 B		5 F	
			U		U				U		O	
6 N	7 A		8 M	I	L	K		9 M	I	10 S	S	I	O	N
11 D	U	B	U	L	A		U		O		T		L	
L		S			L		12 S	H	U	T		E		S
E		13 A	J	14 O	H	N			N		P			
L		L		A		L			T		15 H	A	16 N	G
A		O		I		17 A	18 P	P	L	A	U	S	E	A
		M		L		B		I		L		I		N	T
19 C						E		M		N					I
20 L	I	N	C	O	L	N		V				21 L		V
O						I		I			22 T	I	C	K	E	T
T								L			G			S
H				23 G	U	I	L	T	Y		H			
E								E			T			
S							24 L	I	E	S				

Across
1. Said Absalom had been stealing and was in bad company
8. Mr. Jarvis's first gift to the children
9. ____ House
11. Tomlinson has the brains, John has the voice, but ____ has the heart.
12. Once such a thing is opened, it cannot be ____ again.
13. Stephen's brother, a politician
15. Absalom was sentenced to ____.
17. There is no ____ in prison.
20. Arthur Jarvis read about this American president.
22. A young man stole Stephen's money for his bus ____.
23. Verdict for Absalom
24. John ____ about his son's involvement with Absalom.

Down
2. Stephen's last name
3. The boy tries to learn this language.
4. The Natives were refusing to ride the ____ in protest of increased fares.
5. Nothing is ever quiet except for ____.
6. Says the police are looking for Absalom
7. Stephen's son who has become a criminal
9. Place of spiritual refreshment for Kumalo
10. Pastor who goes to Johannesburg to find his sister (& brother & son)
13. Place where Stephen meets his son
14. Taxi driver
16. John speaks in public for their cause.
18. Place Kumalo found a native girl Absalom had abandoned
19. Gertrude's new ____ symbolize putting on a new life.
21. The____...fall...on the grass and stones of a country that sleeps.

Cry The Beloved Country Crossword 3

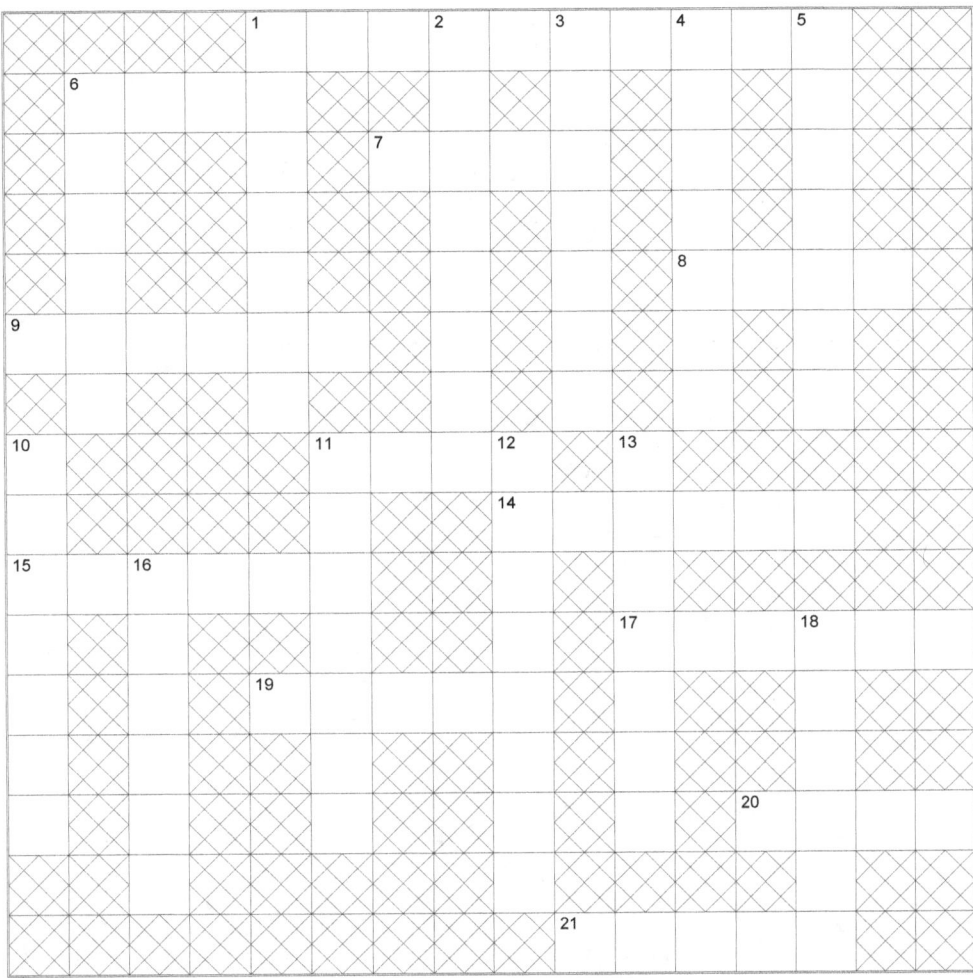

Across
1. Absalom's attorney
6. Place where Stephen meets his son
7. The boy tries to learn this language.
8. John ____ about his son's involvement with Absalom.
9. A young man stole Stephen's money for his bus ____.
11. Absalom was sentenced to ____.
14. Fear impoverishes always, while sorrow may ____.
15. Says the police are looking for Absalom
17. Verdict for Absalom
19. Name for Absalom's son
20. Once such a thing is opened, it cannot be ____ again.
21. Stephen has many of these as his journey begins.

Down
1. Gertrude's new ____ symbolize putting on a new life.
2. Place of spiritual refreshment for Kumalo
3. Cry, the beloved ____, these things are not yet at an end.
4. Stephen's son who has become a criminal
5. Stephen rented a room from her.
6. Arthur; the murdered champion of the Native cause
10. Arthur Jarvis read about this American president.
11. Taxi driver
12. Stephen's sister; he finds her living in immorality
13. The ____'s not that things are broken. The ____ is that they are not mended again.
16. Father Vincent's gift for Absalom
18. The____...fall...on the grass and stones of a country that sleeps.

Cry The Beloved Country Crossword 3 Answer Key

			1 C	A	R	2 M	I	3 C	H	4 A	E	5 L
	6 J	A	I	L		O		O		B		I
		A		O	7 Z	U	L	U		S		T
		R		T		N		N		A		H
		V		H		T		T		8 L	I	E	S
9 T	I	C	K	E	T		A		R		O		B
	S			S			I		Y		M		E
10 L					11 H	A	N	G	12 G	13 T
I					L				14 E	N	R	I	C	H
15 N	D	16 L	E	L	A				R		A
C		A			B				T		17 G	U	I	18 L	T	Y
O		W		19 P	E	T	E	R			E			I
L		Y		N				U			D			G
N		E		I				D			Y		20 S	H	U	T
		R						E					T
								21 F	E	A	R	S

Across
1. Absalom's attorney
6. Place where Stephen meets his son
7. The boy tries to learn this language.
8. John ____ about his son's involvement with Absalom.
9. A young man stole Stephen's money for his bus ____.
11. Absalom was sentenced to ____.
14. Fear impoverishes always, while sorrow may ____.
15. Says the police are looking for Absalom
17. Verdict for Absalom
19. Name for Absalom's son
20. Once such a thing is opened, it cannot be ____ again.
21. Stephen has many of these as his journey begins.

Down
1. Gertrude's new ____ symbolize putting on a new life.
2. Place of spiritual refreshment for Kumalo
3. Cry, the beloved ____, these things are not yet at an end.
4. Stephen's son who has become a criminal
5. Stephen rented a room from her.
6. Arthur; the murdered champion of the Native cause
10. Arthur Jarvis read about this American president.
11. Taxi driver
12. Stephen's sister; he finds her living in immorality
13. The ____'s not that things are broken. The ____ is that they are not mended again.
16. Father Vincent's gift for Absalom
18. The____...fall...on the grass and stones of a country that sleeps.

Cry The Beloved Country Crossword 4

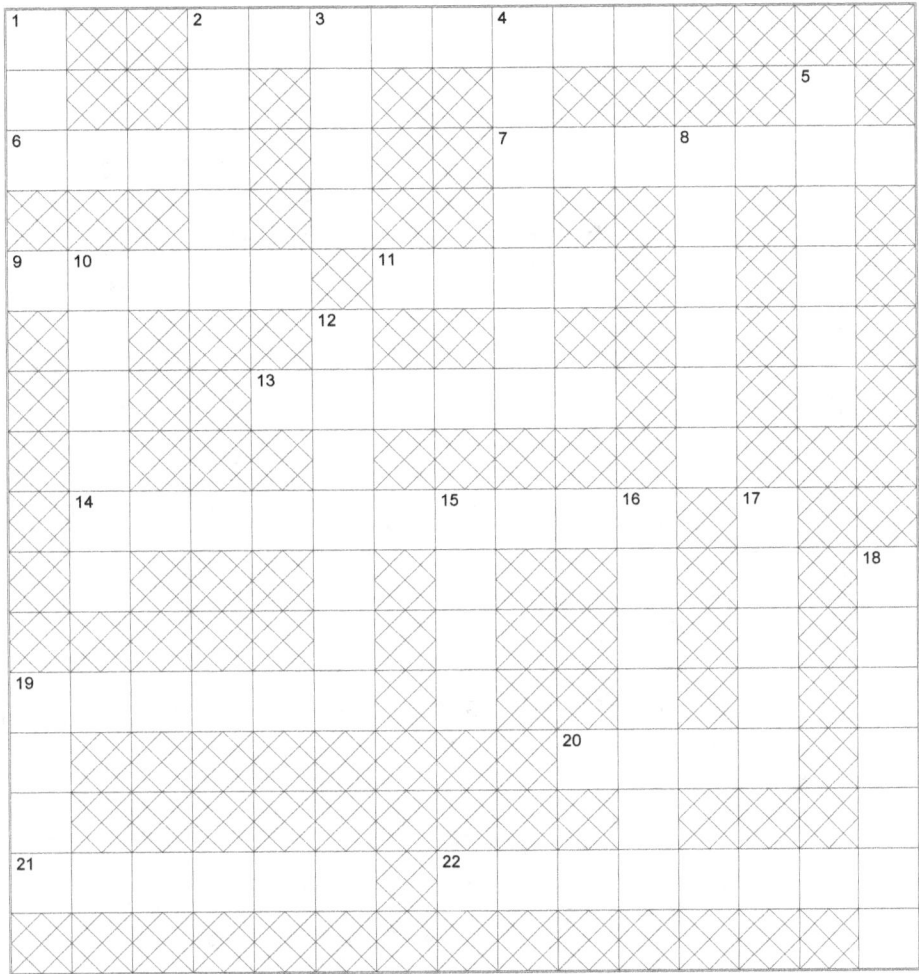

Across

2. Place Kumalo found a native girl Absalom had abandoned
6. Once such a thing is opened, it cannot be ____ again.
7. The ____'s not that things are broken. The ____ is that they are not mended again.
9. Stephen has many of these as his journey begins.
11. John ____ about his son's involvement with Absalom.
13. Father Vincent's gift for Absalom
14. Absalom's attorney
19. Arthur; the murdered champion of the Native cause
20. Stephen's brother, a politician
21. The_____...fall...on the grass and stones of a country that sleeps.
22. Place of spiritual refreshment for Kumalo

Down

1. The Natives were refusing to ride the ____ in protest of increased fares.
2. Name for Absalom's son
3. Mr. Jarvis's first gift to the children
4. Stephen rented a room from her.
5. Says the police are looking for Absalom
8. Verdict for Absalom
10. Fear impoverishes always, while sorrow may ____.
12. John speaks in public for their cause.
15. Absalom was sentenced to ____.
16. Arthur Jarvis read about this American president.
17. Author
18. Priest from England who found a free lawyer for Absalom
19. Place where Stephen meets his son

Cry The Beloved Country Crossword 4 Answer Key

	1 B		2 P		3 M	V	I	L	4 L	E			
	U		E		I				I			5 N	
6 S	H	U	T		L			7 T	R	A	8 G	E	D	Y
			E		K			H			U		L	
9 F	10 E	A	R	S		11 L	I	E	S		I		E	
	N				12 N			B			L		L	
	R			13 L	A	W	Y	E	R		T		A	
	I				T						Y			
	14 C	A	R	M	I	C	15 H	A	16 E	L	17 P		
	H				V		A		I		A		18 V
					E		N		N		T		I
19 J	A	R	V	I	S		G		C		O		N
A							20 J	O	H	N			C
I									O				E
21 L	I	G	H	T	S		22 M	O	U	N	T	A	I	N
													T

Across
2. Place Kumalo found a native girl Absalom had abandoned
6. Once such a thing is opened, it cannot be ____ again.
7. The ____'s not that things are broken. The ____ is that they are not mended again.
9. Stephen has many of these as his journey begins.
11. John ____ about his son's involvement with Absalom.
13. Father Vincent's gift for Absalom
14. Absalom's attorney
19. Arthur; the murdered champion of the Native cause
20. Stephen's brother, a politician
21. The____...fall...on the grass and stones of a country that sleeps.
22. Place of spiritual refreshment for Kumalo

Down
1. The Natives were refusing to ride the ____ in protest of increased fares.
2. Name for Absalom's son
3. Mr. Jarvis's first gift to the children
4. Stephen rented a room from her.
5. Says the police are looking for Absalom
8. Verdict for Absalom
10. Fear impoverishes always, while sorrow may ____.
12. John speaks in public for their cause.
15. Absalom was sentenced to ____.
16. Arthur Jarvis read about this American president.
17. Author
18. Priest from England who found a free lawyer for Absalom
19. Place where Stephen meets his son

Copyrighted

Cry The Beloved Country

PIMVILLE	TICKET	FOOLS	JARVIS	STEPHEN
ENRICH	LAWYER	TRAGEDY	PATON	LIES
ABSALOM	CLOTHES	FREE SPACE	KUMALO	HANG
JAMES	BUS	MISSION	UMFUNDISI	COUNTRY
GERTRUDE	APPLAUSE	MILK	MKIZE	MSIMANGU

Cry The Beloved Country

GUILTY	MOUNTAIN	DUBULA	SHUT	JOHN
JAIL	LIGHTS	ZULU	LINCOLN	NDLELA
HLABENI	VINCENT	FREE SPACE	CARMICHAEL	FEARS
NATIVES	LITHEBE	MSIMANGU	MKIZE	MILK
APPLAUSE	GERTRUDE	COUNTRY	UMFUNDISI	MISSION

Cry The Beloved Country

MKIZE	LINCOLN	MOUNTAIN	JARVIS	ABSALOM
APPLAUSE	UMFUNDISI	FEARS	CLOTHES	MILK
SHUT	LIGHTS	FREE SPACE	BUS	MISSION
CARMICHAEL	JOHANNESBURG	DUBULA	HLABENI	FOOLS
MSIMANGU	ZULU	ENRICH	LITHEBE	PETER

Cry The Beloved Country

LIES	JAMES	VINCENT	NATIVES	KUMALO
GUILTY	JOHN	JAIL	PIMVILLE	TRAGEDY
PATON	HANG	FREE SPACE	STEPHEN	LAWYER
NDLELA	TICKET	PETER	LITHEBE	ENRICH
ZULU	MSIMANGU	FOOLS	HLABENI	DUBULA

Cry The Beloved Country

NATIVES	HLABENI	JOHANNESBURG	CLOTHES	ENRICH
GERTRUDE	MSIMANGU	STEPHEN	MILK	LIGHTS
VINCENT	PATON	FREE SPACE	MISSION	NDLELA
JOHN	MOUNTAIN	APPLAUSE	CARMICHAEL	DUBULA
MKIZE	FOOLS	KUMALO	JAIL	TICKET

Cry The Beloved Country

PETER	SHUT	PIMVILLE	GUILTY	LIES
ZULU	COUNTRY	JAMES	ABSALOM	LITHEBE
BUS	JARVIS	FREE SPACE	LAWYER	HANG
FEARS	TRAGEDY	TICKET	JAIL	KUMALO
FOOLS	MKIZE	DUBULA	CARMICHAEL	APPLAUSE

Cry The Beloved Country

HANG	STEPHEN	CARMICHAEL	COUNTRY	LINCOLN
LIES	GUILTY	PATON	JOHANNESBURG	LIGHTS
NDLELA	MOUNTAIN	FREE SPACE	MSIMANGU	PETER
BUS	UMFUNDISI	DUBULA	MKIZE	CLOTHES
ABSALOM	JAIL	JAMES	TICKET	FEARS

Cry The Beloved Country

KUMALO	SHUT	JOHN	NATIVES	HLABENI
APPLAUSE	TRAGEDY	LAWYER	GERTRUDE	VINCENT
JARVIS	MILK	FREE SPACE	LITHEBE	ZULU
MISSION	FOOLS	FEARS	TICKET	JAMES
JAIL	ABSALOM	CLOTHES	MKIZE	DUBULA

Cry The Beloved Country

MILK	VINCENT	HLABENI	NATIVES	HANG
MKIZE	LAWYER	LITHEBE	KUMALO	FOOLS
GUILTY	PETER	FREE SPACE	CLOTHES	STEPHEN
ABSALOM	ENRICH	PIMVILLE	FEARS	NDLELA
TRAGEDY	UMFUNDISI	PATON	BUS	JAMES

Cry The Beloved Country

JARVIS	CARMICHAEL	LINCOLN	LIGHTS	MOUNTAIN
DUBULA	TICKET	JOHANNESBURG	APPLAUSE	ZULU
COUNTRY	LIES	FREE SPACE	JAIL	MSIMANGU
JOHN	GERTRUDE	JAMES	BUS	PATON
UMFUNDISI	TRAGEDY	NDLELA	FEARS	PIMVILLE

Cry The Beloved Country

SHUT	ENRICH	FEARS	HANG	JARVIS
LAWYER	CLOTHES	PETER	MOUNTAIN	BUS
PATON	NATIVES	FREE SPACE	UMFUNDISI	KUMALO
COUNTRY	PIMVILLE	GERTRUDE	TICKET	GUILTY
JAMES	LIES	ABSALOM	TRAGEDY	ZULU

Cry The Beloved Country

NDLELA	JOHN	LITHEBE	STEPHEN	JAIL
LIGHTS	LINCOLN	HLABENI	FOOLS	MKIZE
VINCENT	MSIMANGU	FREE SPACE	MILK	CARMICHAEL
MISSION	JOHANNESBURG	ZULU	TRAGEDY	ABSALOM
LIES	JAMES	GUILTY	TICKET	GERTRUDE

Cry The Beloved Country

COUNTRY	CARMICHAEL	JARVIS	TRAGEDY	MOUNTAIN
MILK	MKIZE	HANG	LIGHTS	JAIL
NATIVES	SHUT	FREE SPACE	ABSALOM	UMFUNDISI
TICKET	APPLAUSE	PIMVILLE	KUMALO	ENRICH
LIES	JAMES	JOHANNESBURG	CLOTHES	STEPHEN

Cry The Beloved Country

GERTRUDE	LINCOLN	PETER	VINCENT	MSIMANGU
JOHN	FEARS	PATON	LAWYER	DUBULA
BUS	NDLELA	FREE SPACE	FOOLS	LITHEBE
ZULU	HLABENI	STEPHEN	CLOTHES	JOHANNESBURG
JAMES	LIES	ENRICH	KUMALO	PIMVILLE

Cry The Beloved Country

LIGHTS	JARVIS	JAIL	UMFUNDISI	NATIVES
SHUT	NDLELA	APPLAUSE	HANG	MILK
FOOLS	LITHEBE	FREE SPACE	COUNTRY	HLABENI
ABSALOM	PATON	MISSION	TRAGEDY	LIES
JOHN	FEARS	MKIZE	PIMVILLE	BUS

Cry The Beloved Country

KUMALO	MSIMANGU	LINCOLN	JOHANNESBURG	ENRICH
GUILTY	LAWYER	CLOTHES	VINCENT	JAMES
GERTRUDE	PETER	FREE SPACE	TICKET	ZULU
MOUNTAIN	STEPHEN	BUS	PIMVILLE	MKIZE
FEARS	JOHN	LIES	TRAGEDY	MISSION

Cry The Beloved Country

CARMICHAEL	HANG	NDLELA	LIGHTS	COUNTRY
CLOTHES	DUBULA	JAIL	MISSION	MSIMANGU
FOOLS	PIMVILLE	FREE SPACE	BUS	TRAGEDY
MKIZE	TICKET	STEPHEN	GUILTY	PETER
NATIVES	APPLAUSE	ZULU	JOHANNESBURG	KUMALO

Cry The Beloved Country

JOHN	LAWYER	ABSALOM	ENRICH	HLABENI
GERTRUDE	PATON	MOUNTAIN	JARVIS	FEARS
LIES	UMFUNDISI	FREE SPACE	JAMES	VINCENT
LITHEBE	MILK	KUMALO	JOHANNESBURG	ZULU
APPLAUSE	NATIVES	PETER	GUILTY	STEPHEN

Cry The Beloved Country

BUS	PATON	CLOTHES	JAIL	TICKET
CARMICHAEL	MILK	GERTRUDE	JOHANNESBURG	HLABENI
LIGHTS	MKIZE	FREE SPACE	JOHN	SHUT
COUNTRY	ABSALOM	HANG	LINCOLN	NDLELA
ZULU	TRAGEDY	DUBULA	GUILTY	LITHEBE

Cry The Beloved Country

MOUNTAIN	APPLAUSE	NATIVES	UMFUNDISI	KUMALO
FOOLS	LIES	PETER	MISSION	JARVIS
VINCENT	ENRICH	FREE SPACE	MSIMANGU	LAWYER
STEPHEN	PIMVILLE	LITHEBE	GUILTY	DUBULA
TRAGEDY	ZULU	NDLELA	LINCOLN	HANG

Cry The Beloved Country

HANG	MISSION	JAIL	KUMALO	MKIZE
PIMVILLE	NDLELA	CLOTHES	JAMES	MILK
PETER	COUNTRY	FREE SPACE	LINCOLN	DUBULA
SHUT	GERTRUDE	TRAGEDY	ZULU	LIES
PATON	MSIMANGU	STEPHEN	UMFUNDISI	TICKET

Cry The Beloved Country

JOHN	JOHANNESBURG	ENRICH	ABSALOM	CARMICHAEL
LAWYER	NATIVES	FEARS	LITHEBE	GUILTY
VINCENT	JARVIS	FREE SPACE	FOOLS	MOUNTAIN
APPLAUSE	HLABENI	TICKET	UMFUNDISI	STEPHEN
MSIMANGU	PATON	LIES	ZULU	TRAGEDY

Cry The Beloved Country

PATON	JAIL	SHUT	COUNTRY	UMFUNDISI
HANG	APPLAUSE	JAMES	KUMALO	VINCENT
LIGHTS	ZULU	FREE SPACE	FOOLS	CLOTHES
CARMICHAEL	FEARS	LAWYER	DUBULA	BUS
PETER	JOHANNESBURG	GERTRUDE	LITHEBE	JOHN

Cry The Beloved Country

MSIMANGU	NDLELA	STEPHEN	PIMVILLE	MISSION
TICKET	LIES	ABSALOM	ENRICH	TRAGEDY
JARVIS	NATIVES	FREE SPACE	MILK	MKIZE
HLABENI	MOUNTAIN	JOHN	LITHEBE	GERTRUDE
JOHANNESBURG	PETER	BUS	DUBULA	LAWYER

Cry The Beloved Country

LINCOLN	PETER	DUBULA	JAMES	JOHANNESBURG
NATIVES	GERTRUDE	LAWYER	JOHN	COUNTRY
NDLELA	HANG	FREE SPACE	FEARS	MILK
VINCENT	HLABENI	TICKET	MKIZE	JAIL
FOOLS	ENRICH	MOUNTAIN	ABSALOM	MSIMANGU

Cry The Beloved Country

MISSION	LITHEBE	GUILTY	JARVIS	SHUT
KUMALO	APPLAUSE	TRAGEDY	ZULU	PIMVILLE
UMFUNDISI	LIES	FREE SPACE	PATON	CARMICHAEL
STEPHEN	CLOTHES	MSIMANGU	ABSALOM	MOUNTAIN
ENRICH	FOOLS	JAIL	MKIZE	TICKET

Cry The Beloved Country

LIGHTS	ABSALOM	MSIMANGU	COUNTRY	GUILTY
KUMALO	UMFUNDISI	APPLAUSE	NATIVES	STEPHEN
DUBULA	FEARS	FREE SPACE	LIES	LITHEBE
CARMICHAEL	ENRICH	TRAGEDY	ZULU	TICKET
MILK	SHUT	VINCENT	PATON	HANG

Cry The Beloved Country

PIMVILLE	JARVIS	JOHANNESBURG	JOHN	MKIZE
JAIL	HLABENI	GERTRUDE	MISSION	BUS
FOOLS	LINCOLN	FREE SPACE	JAMES	LAWYER
MOUNTAIN	NDLELA	HANG	PATON	VINCENT
SHUT	MILK	TICKET	ZULU	TRAGEDY

Cry The Beloved Country

MSIMANGU	MOUNTAIN	PATON	ZULU	LAWYER
BUS	ENRICH	LIGHTS	DUBULA	HANG
MKIZE	CARMICHAEL	FREE SPACE	VINCENT	TRAGEDY
KUMALO	PIMVILLE	JOHN	GERTRUDE	TICKET
LINCOLN	UMFUNDISI	MISSION	JAMES	FOOLS

Cry The Beloved Country

MILK	JOHANNESBURG	CLOTHES	NATIVES	FEARS
APPLAUSE	HLABENI	LIES	GUILTY	STEPHEN
ABSALOM	COUNTRY	FREE SPACE	LITHEBE	JARVIS
NDLELA	PETER	FOOLS	JAMES	MISSION
UMFUNDISI	LINCOLN	TICKET	GERTRUDE	JOHN

Cry The Beloved Country

LITHEBE	ABSALOM	JAIL	DUBULA	JOHANNESBURG
BUS	JAMES	HANG	FOOLS	CLOTHES
MISSION	ENRICH	FREE SPACE	NATIVES	CARMICHAEL
JOHN	FEARS	GUILTY	APPLAUSE	VINCENT
LIES	STEPHEN	GERTRUDE	TRAGEDY	LIGHTS

Cry The Beloved Country

PETER	MSIMANGU	MKIZE	PATON	PIMVILLE
MILK	HLABENI	KUMALO	SHUT	LINCOLN
TICKET	UMFUNDISI	FREE SPACE	MOUNTAIN	LAWYER
JARVIS	COUNTRY	LIGHTS	TRAGEDY	GERTRUDE
STEPHEN	LIES	VINCENT	APPLAUSE	GUILTY

Cry Beloved Vocabulary Word List

No.	Word	Clue/Definition
1.	ABATING	Lessening
2.	ABIDE	To remain in place
3.	ACCOMPLICES	Those who aid a lawbreaker in a criminal act
4.	AMENDED	Improved
5.	ARRAY	Display
6.	ASPIRATION	A strong desire for high achievement; ambition
7.	ASTONISHED	To fill with sudden wonder or amazement
8.	ASTRAY	Away from the correct path or direction
9.	BEREAVEMENT	Grief over someone's death
10.	BEWILDERS	Confuses or befuddles
11.	BOYCOTT	To abstain from using, buying, or dealing with as a form of protest
12.	BRACKEN	A widespread, often weedy fern
13.	CLEAVE	To split with a sharp instrument
14.	COMPELLED	Forced to action
15.	CONGENIAL	Suited to one's needs or nature; agreeable
16.	CONSTRAINT	Awkwardness
17.	CONVEY	To communicate or make known
18.	CORRUPTED	Marked by immorality and perversion
19.	CULPABLE	Deserving of blame or censure as being wrong
20.	CUNNING	Subtle; deceitful
21.	DELL	A small, secluded, wooded valley
22.	DELUSION	A false belief or opinion
23.	DESOLATION	Barrenness; dreariness; hopelessness
24.	DOGGEDLY	Stubbornly persevering; tenaciously
25.	DUBIOUS	Doubtful
26.	ENRAPT	To fill with rapture or delight
27.	EXPLOITATION	Taking advantage of people or a situation for monetary gain
28.	EXPOSITION	A statement or rhetorical discourse intended to give information about or explain difficult material
29.	FIDELITY	Faithfulness to obligations, or duties
30.	GRATIFY	To please or satisfy
31.	HINDRANCE	An impediment; something that gets in the way
32.	INCORRUPTIBLE	Incapable of being swayed to do anything immoral, illegal, or unethical
33.	INELUCTABLE	Not to be avoided or escaped; inevitable
34.	INEVITABLE	Impossible to avoid or prevent
35.	IRRESOLUTE	Unsure of how to act or proceed; undecided
36.	IRRITATE	Annoy; bother
37.	KLOOF	Ravine
38.	KRAAL	A rural village
39.	LINGO	Language
40.	LORRY	A motor truck
41.	MENACE	A possible danger; a threat
42.	MOULD	General shape or form
43.	MUNICIPALITY	A political unit, such as a city or town, incorporated for local self-government
44.	NEGROPHILE	One friendly to Negros and their interests
45.	OBLIGING	Willing to do a service or favor for
46.	OBSCURE	Hidden; not clearly understood

Cry Beloved Vocabulary Word List Continued

No.	Word	Clue/Definition
47.	PARSON	A member of the clergy, especially a Protestant minister
48.	PERMISSIBLE	Permitted; allowable
49.	PERPLEXED	Confused or troubled with uncertainty or doubt
50.	PILGRIMAGE	A long journey or search
51.	PRELUDE	Introduction
52.	PROVISIONALLY	Temporarily
53.	REPENT	To feel such regret for past conduct as to change one's mind regarding it
54.	REPROACHFULLY	Expressing blame
55.	REVERIE	Daydream
56.	SELF-DENUNCIATION	Self-accusation; self-condemnation
57.	SOMBRE	Dark; gloomy; serious; grave
58.	SUBSIDIES	Monetary assistance granted by a government
59.	SULLENLY	Showing a brooding ill humor
60.	SUMMON	Gather together
61.	SYMPOSIUM	A meeting or conference for discussion of a topic
62.	TIERS	One of a series of rows placed one above another
63.	TRAVAIL	Work; painful effort; toil
64.	TREMULOUS	Marked by trembling, quivering, or shaking
65.	UNENDURABLE	Unbearable
66.	VACILLATE	To swing indecisively from one course of action or opinion to another
67.	VAGABONDS	People without a permanent home who move from place to place
68.	VERANDAHS	A porch or balcony, usually roofed, often partly enclosed, extending along the outside of a building
69.	VICIOUSLY	Aggressively; savagely
70.	WARDER	A guard

Cry Beloved Vocabulary Fill In The Blanks 1

1. People without a permanent home who move from place to place
2. A meeting or conference for discussion of a topic
3. To fill with sudden wonder or amazement
4. One of a series of rows placed one above another
5. Unsure of how to act or proceed; undecided
6. Introduction
7. Doubtful
8. Aggressively; savagely
9. An impediment; something that gets in the way
10. To please or satisfy
11. Those who aid a lawbreaker in a criminal act
12. To communicate or make known
13. Dark; gloomy; serious; grave
14. Faithfulness to obligations, or duties
15. A political unit, such as a city or town, incorporated for local self-government
16. To fill with rapture or delight
17. A strong desire for high achievement; ambition
18. Barrenness; dreariness; hopelessness
19. A statement or rhetorical discourse intended to give information about or explain difficult material
20. Incapable of being swayed to do anything immoral, illegal, or unethical

Cry Beloved Vocabulary Fill In The Blanks 1 Answer Key

VAGABONDS	1. People without a permanent home who move from place to place
SYMPOSIUM	2. A meeting or conference for discussion of a topic
ASTONISHED	3. To fill with sudden wonder or amazement
TIERS	4. One of a series of rows placed one above another
IRRESOLUTE	5. Unsure of how to act or proceed; undecided
PRELUDE	6. Introduction
DUBIOUS	7. Doubtful
VICIOUSLY	8. Aggressively; savagely
HINDRANCE	9. An impediment; something that gets in the way
GRATIFY	10. To please or satisfy
ACCOMPLICES	11. Those who aid a lawbreaker in a criminal act
CONVEY	12. To communicate or make known
SOMBRE	13. Dark; gloomy; serious; grave
FIDELITY	14. Faithfulness to obligations, or duties
MUNICIPALITY	15. A political unit, such as a city or town, incorporated for local self-government
ENRAPT	16. To fill with rapture or delight
ASPIRATION	17. A strong desire for high achievement; ambition
DESOLATION	18. Barrenness; dreariness; hopelessness
EXPOSITION	19. A statement or rhetorical discourse intended to give information about or explain difficult material
INCORRUPTIBLE	20. Incapable of being swayed to do anything immoral, illegal, or unethical

Cry Beloved Vocabulary Fill In The Blanks 2

_____

1. Away from the correct path or direction

_____

2. Barrenness; dreariness; hopelessness

_____

3. Awkwardness

_____

4. A false belief or opinion

_____

5. Self-accusation; self-condemnation

_____

6. A guard

_____

7. Temporarily

_____

8. A widespread, often weedy fern

_____

9. An impediment; something that gets in the way

_____

10. Suited to one's needs or nature; agreeable

_____

11. To split with a sharp instrument

_____

12. Gather together

_____

13. A member of the clergy, especially a Protestant minister

_____

14. Taking advantage of people or a situation for monetary gain

15. A meeting or conference for discussion of a topic

_____

16. One of a series of rows placed one above another

_____

17. Monetary assistance granted by a government

_____

18. Lessening

_____

19. General shape or form

_____

20. Improved

Cry Beloved Vocabulary Fill In The Blanks 2 Answer Key

ASTRAY	1. Away from the correct path or direction
DESOLATION	2. Barrenness; dreariness; hopelessness
CONSTRAINT	3. Awkwardness
DELUSION	4. A false belief or opinion
SELF-DENUNCIATION	5. Self-accusation; self-condemnation
WARDER	6. A guard
PROVISIONALLY	7. Temporarily
BRACKEN	8. A widespread, often weedy fern
HINDRANCE	9. An impediment; something that gets in the way
CONGENIAL	10. Suited to one's needs or nature; agreeable
CLEAVE	11. To split with a sharp instrument
SUMMON	12. Gather together
PARSON	13. A member of the clergy, especially a Protestant minister
EXPLOITATION	14. Taking advantage of people or a situation for monetary gain
SYMPOSIUM	15. A meeting or conference for discussion of a topic
TIERS	16. One of a series of rows placed one above another
SUBSIDIES	17. Monetary assistance granted by a government
ABATING	18. Lessening
MOULD	19. General shape or form
AMENDED	20. Improved

Cry Beloved Vocabulary Fill In The Blanks 3

1. To swing indecisively from one course of action or opinion to another
2. Showing a brooding ill humor
3. Introduction
4. A statement or rhetorical discourse intended to give information about or explain difficult material
5. Faithfulness to obligations, or duties
6. Away from the correct path or direction
7. Display
8. A false belief or opinion
9. Not to be avoided or escaped; inevitable
10. Annoy; bother
11. Ravine
12. Work; painful effort; toil
13. Gather together
14. Self-accusation; self-condemnation
15. A political unit, such as a city or town, incorporated for local self-government
16. Confuses or befuddles
17. Incapable of being swayed to do anything immoral, illegal, or unethical
18. Suited to one's needs or nature; agreeable
19. Temporarily
20. A strong desire for high achievement; ambition

Cry Beloved Vocabulary Fill In The Blanks 3 Answer Key

VACILLATE	1. To swing indecisively from one course of action or opinion to another
SULLENLY	2. Showing a brooding ill humor
PRELUDE	3. Introduction
EXPOSITION	4. A statement or rhetorical discourse intended to give information about or explain difficult material
FIDELITY	5. Faithfulness to obligations, or duties
ASTRAY	6. Away from the correct path or direction
ARRAY	7. Display
DELUSION	8. A false belief or opinion
INELUCTABLE	9. Not to be avoided or escaped; inevitable
IRRITATE	10. Annoy; bother
KLOOF	11. Ravine
TRAVAIL	12. Work; painful effort; toil
SUMMON	13. Gather together
SELF-DENUNCIATION	14. Self-accusation; self-condemnation
MUNICIPALITY	15. A political unit, such as a city or town, incorporated for local self-government
BEWILDERS	16. Confuses or befuddles
INCORRUPTIBLE	17. Incapable of being swayed to do anything immoral, illegal, or unethical
CONGENIAL	18. Suited to one's needs or nature; agreeable
PROVISIONALLY	19. Temporarily
ASPIRATION	20. A strong desire for high achievement; ambition

Cry Beloved Vocabulary Fill In The Blanks 4

_____ 1. Subtle; deceitful

_____ 2. Doubtful

_____ 3. A member of the clergy, especially a Protestant minister

_____ 4. Grief over someone's death

_____ 5. Improved

_____ 6. Aggressively; savagely

_____ 7. Ravine

_____ 8. Marked by trembling, quivering, or shaking

_____ 9. To please or satisfy

_____ 10. A false belief or opinion

_____ 11. An impediment; something that gets in the way

_____ 12. Confuses or befuddles

_____ 13. Monetary assistance granted by a government

_____ 14. Unsure of how to act or proceed; undecided

_____ 15. A widespread, often weedy fern

_____ 16. Faithfulness to obligations, or duties

_____ 17. Incapable of being swayed to do anything immoral, illegal, or unethical

_____ 18. To swing indecisively from one course of action or opinion to another

_____ 19. To fill with sudden wonder or amazement

_____ 20. One friendly to Negros and their interests

Cry Beloved Vocabulary Fill In The Blanks 4 Answer Key

CUNNING	1. Subtle; deceitful
DUBIOUS	2. Doubtful
PARSON	3. A member of the clergy, especially a Protestant minister
BEREAVEMENT	4. Grief over someone's death
AMENDED	5. Improved
VICIOUSLY	6. Aggressively; savagely
KLOOF	7. Ravine
TREMULOUS	8. Marked by trembling, quivering, or shaking
GRATIFY	9. To please or satisfy
DELUSION	10. A false belief or opinion
HINDRANCE	11. An impediment; something that gets in the way
BEWILDERS	12. Confuses or befuddles
SUBSIDIES	13. Monetary assistance granted by a government
IRRESOLUTE	14. Unsure of how to act or proceed; undecided
BRACKEN	15. A widespread, often weedy fern
FIDELITY	16. Faithfulness to obligations, or duties
INCORRUPTIBLE	17. Incapable of being swayed to do anything immoral, illegal, or unethical
VACILLATE	18. To swing indecisively from one course of action or opinion to another
ASTONISHED	19. To fill with sudden wonder or amazement
NEGROPHILE	20. One friendly to Negros and their interests

Cry Beloved Vocabulary Matching 1

___ 1. PARSON
___ 2. SUMMON
___ 3. COMPELLED
___ 4. MENACE
___ 5. CLEAVE
___ 6. IRRESOLUTE
___ 7. SELF-DENUNCIATION
___ 8. MOULD
___ 9. CONGENIAL
___ 10. REPROACHFULLY
___ 11. VICIOUSLY
___ 12. EXPLOITATION
___ 13. SOMBRE
___ 14. VAGABONDS
___ 15. SYMPOSIUM
___ 16. ASPIRATION
___ 17. DESOLATION
___ 18. CONVEY
___ 19. PERPLEXED
___ 20. OBLIGING
___ 21. DUBIOUS
___ 22. BEWILDERS
___ 23. IRRITATE
___ 24. ASTRAY
___ 25. REVERIE

A. Confused or troubled with uncertainty or doubt
B. Dark; gloomy; serious; grave
C. A meeting or conference for discussion of a topic
D. Away from the correct path or direction
E. Unsure of how to act or proceed; undecided
F. Forced to action
G. People without a permanent home who move from place to place
H. Annoy; bother
I. Self-accusation; self-condemnation
J. Doubtful
K. To communicate or make known
L. Expressing blame
M. Gather together
N. A possible danger; a threat
O. Aggressively; savagely
P. Willing to do a service or favor for
Q. Barrenness; dreariness; hopelessness
R. General shape or form
S. Daydream
T. Confuses or befuddles
U. Taking advantage of people or a situation for monetary gain
V. A member of the clergy, especially a Protestant minister
W. A strong desire for high achievement; ambition
X. Suited to one's needs or nature; agreeable
Y. To split with a sharp instrument

Cry Beloved Vocabulary Matching 1 Answer Key

V - 1. PARSON		A. Confused or troubled with uncertainty or doubt
M - 2. SUMMON		B. Dark; gloomy; serious; grave
F - 3. COMPELLED		C. A meeting or conference for discussion of a topic
N - 4. MENACE		D. Away from the correct path or direction
Y - 5. CLEAVE		E. Unsure of how to act or proceed; undecided
E - 6. IRRESOLUTE		F. Forced to action
I - 7. SELF-DENUNCIATION		G. People without a permanent home who move from place to place
R - 8. MOULD		H. Annoy; bother
X - 9. CONGENIAL		I. Self-accusation; self-condemnation
L - 10. REPROACHFULLY		J. Doubtful
O - 11. VICIOUSLY		K. To communicate or make known
U - 12. EXPLOITATION		L. Expressing blame
B - 13. SOMBRE		M. Gather together
G - 14. VAGABONDS		N. A possible danger; a threat
C - 15. SYMPOSIUM		O. Aggressively; savagely
W - 16. ASPIRATION		P. Willing to do a service or favor for
Q - 17. DESOLATION		Q. Barrenness; dreariness; hopelessness
K - 18. CONVEY		R. General shape or form
A - 19. PERPLEXED		S. Daydream
P - 20. OBLIGING		T. Confuses or befuddles
J - 21. DUBIOUS		U. Taking advantage of people or a situation for monetary gain
T - 22. BEWILDERS		V. A member of the clergy, especially a Protestant minister
H - 23. IRRITATE		W. A strong desire for high achievement; ambition
D - 24. ASTRAY		X. Suited to one's needs or nature; agreeable
S - 25. REVERIE		Y. To split with a sharp instrument

Cry Beloved Vocabulary Matching 2

___ 1. VICIOUSLY
___ 2. INCORRUPTIBLE
___ 3. WARDER
___ 4. PILGRIMAGE
___ 5. DELUSION
___ 6. KLOOF
___ 7. ABATING
___ 8. CULPABLE
___ 9. VERANDAHS
___10. ABIDE
___11. COMPELLED
___12. TREMULOUS
___13. MENACE
___14. CLEAVE
___15. ENRAPT
___16. BOYCOTT
___17. PERMISSIBLE
___18. PROVISIONALLY
___19. OBSCURE
___20. REVERIE
___21. NEGROPHILE
___22. VAGABONDS
___23. LINGO
___24. BEREAVEMENT
___25. ARRAY

A. Daydream
B. Deserving of blame or censure as being wrong
C. Language
D. To split with a sharp instrument
E. Marked by trembling, quivering, or shaking
F. Forced to action
G. To remain in place
H. One friendly to Negros and their interests
I. Permitted; allowable
J. People without a permanent home who move from place to place
K. To fill with rapture or delight
L. Display
M. Ravine
N. A long journey or search
O. A porch or balcony, usually roofed, often partly enclosed, extending along the outside of a building
P. Aggressively; savagely
Q. Lessening
R. To abstain from using, buying, or dealing with as a form of protest
S. Hidden; not clearly understood
T. A false belief or opinion
U. Incapable of being swayed to do anything immoral, illegal, or unethical
V. Temporarily
W. A possible danger; a threat
X. Grief over someone's death
Y. A guard

Cry Beloved Vocabulary Matching 2 Answer Key

P - 1. VICIOUSLY
U - 2. INCORRUPTIBLE
Y - 3. WARDER
N - 4. PILGRIMAGE
T - 5. DELUSION
M - 6. KLOOF
Q - 7. ABATING
B - 8. CULPABLE
O - 9. VERANDAHS
G - 10. ABIDE
F - 11. COMPELLED
E - 12. TREMULOUS
W - 13. MENACE
D - 14. CLEAVE
K - 15. ENRAPT
R - 16. BOYCOTT
I - 17. PERMISSIBLE
V - 18. PROVISIONALLY
S - 19. OBSCURE
A - 20. REVERIE
H - 21. NEGROPHILE
J - 22. VAGABONDS
C - 23. LINGO
X - 24. BEREAVEMENT
L - 25. ARRAY

A. Daydream
B. Deserving of blame or censure as being wrong
C. Language
D. To split with a sharp instrument
E. Marked by trembling, quivering, or shaking
F. Forced to action
G. To remain in place
H. One friendly to Negros and their interests
I. Permitted; allowable
J. People without a permanent home who move from place to place
K. To fill with rapture or delight
L. Display
M. Ravine
N. A long journey or search
O. A porch or balcony, usually roofed, often partly enclosed, extending along the outside of a building
P. Aggressively; savagely
Q. Lessening
R. To abstain from using, buying, or dealing with as a form of protest
S. Hidden; not clearly understood
T. A false belief or opinion
U. Incapable of being swayed to do anything immoral, illegal, or unethical
V. Temporarily
W. A possible danger; a threat
X. Grief over someone's death
Y. A guard

Cry Beloved Vocabulary Matching 3

___ 1. EXPLOITATION
___ 2. MENACE
___ 3. PARSON
___ 4. KLOOF
___ 5. REPROACHFULLY
___ 6. SOMBRE
___ 7. REVERIE
___ 8. OBSCURE
___ 9. CONVEY
___ 10. PROVISIONALLY
___ 11. BEREAVEMENT
___ 12. DUBIOUS
___ 13. DESOLATION
___ 14. TREMULOUS
___ 15. PERPLEXED
___ 16. INELUCTABLE
___ 17. MOULD
___ 18. PERMISSIBLE
___ 19. MUNICIPALITY
___ 20. LINGO
___ 21. ABIDE
___ 22. BRACKEN
___ 23. GRATIFY
___ 24. DELL
___ 25. VAGABONDS

A. Ravine
B. A small, secluded, wooded valley
C. Permitted; allowable
D. A widespread, often weedy fern
E. Marked by trembling, quivering, or shaking
F. People without a permanent home who move from place to place
G. Doubtful
H. Barrenness; dreariness; hopelessness
I. A political unit, such as a city or town, incorporated for local self-government
J. Confused or troubled with uncertainty or doubt
K. Hidden; not clearly understood
L. To remain in place
M. A possible danger; a threat
N. Temporarily
O. Grief over someone's death
P. Expressing blame
Q. Taking advantage of people or a situation for monetary gain
R. Not to be avoided or escaped; inevitable
S. General shape or form
T. To please or satisfy
U. Dark; gloomy; serious; grave
V. Language
W. To communicate or make known
X. Daydream
Y. A member of the clergy, especially a Protestant minister

Cry Beloved Vocabulary Matching 3 Answer Key

Q - 1.	EXPLOITATION	A. Ravine
M - 2.	MENACE	B. A small, secluded, wooded valley
Y - 3.	PARSON	C. Permitted; allowable
A - 4.	KLOOF	D. A widespread, often weedy fern
P - 5.	REPROACHFULLY	E. Marked by trembling, quivering, or shaking
U - 6.	SOMBRE	F. People without a permanent home who move from place to place
X - 7.	REVERIE	G. Doubtful
K - 8.	OBSCURE	H. Barrenness; dreariness; hopelessness
W - 9.	CONVEY	I. A political unit, such as a city or town, incorporated for local self-government
N - 10.	PROVISIONALLY	J. Confused or troubled with uncertainty or doubt
O - 11.	BEREAVEMENT	K. Hidden; not clearly understood
G - 12.	DUBIOUS	L. To remain in place
H - 13.	DESOLATION	M. A possible danger; a threat
E - 14.	TREMULOUS	N. Temporarily
J - 15.	PERPLEXED	O. Grief over someone's death
R - 16.	INELUCTABLE	P. Expressing blame
S - 17.	MOULD	Q. Taking advantage of people or a situation for monetary gain
C - 18.	PERMISSIBLE	R. Not to be avoided or escaped; inevitable
I - 19.	MUNICIPALITY	S. General shape or form
V - 20.	LINGO	T. To please or satisfy
L - 21.	ABIDE	U. Dark; gloomy; serious; grave
D - 22.	BRACKEN	V. Language
T - 23.	GRATIFY	W. To communicate or make known
B - 24.	DELL	X. Daydream
F - 25.	VAGABONDS	Y. A member of the clergy, especially a Protestant minister

Cry Beloved Vocabulary Matching 4

___ 1. VERANDAHS
___ 2. COMPELLED
___ 3. MUNICIPALITY
___ 4. INELUCTABLE
___ 5. ARRAY
___ 6. HINDRANCE
___ 7. MOULD
___ 8. VICIOUSLY
___ 9. ASTRAY
___ 10. VACILLATE
___ 11. CULPABLE
___ 12. CUNNING
___ 13. CONVEY
___ 14. LINGO
___ 15. LORRY
___ 16. ACCOMPLICES
___ 17. SYMPOSIUM
___ 18. BOYCOTT
___ 19. INCORRUPTIBLE
___ 20. DOGGEDLY
___ 21. TREMULOUS
___ 22. EXPOSITION
___ 23. FIDELITY
___ 24. BEREAVEMENT
___ 25. SUMMON

A. Forced to action
B. Display
C. Away from the correct path or direction
D. Those who aid a lawbreaker in a criminal act
E. Language
F. General shape or form
G. Marked by trembling, quivering, or shaking
H. Subtle; deceitful
I. A statement or rhetorical discourse intended to give information about or explain difficult material
J. A porch or balcony, usually roofed, often partly enclosed, extending along the outside of a building
K. To communicate or make known
L. To abstain from using, buying, or dealing with as a form of protest
M. Gather together
N. Stubbornly persevering; tenaciously
O. Faithfulness to obligations, or duties
P. An impediment; something that gets in the way
Q. A meeting or conference for discussion of a topic
R. To swing indecisively from one course of action or opinion to another
S. Not to be avoided or escaped; inevitable
T. A political unit, such as a city or town, incorporated for local self-government
U. Aggressively; savagely
V. A motor truck
W. Incapable of being swayed to do anything immoral, illegal, or unethical
X. Deserving of blame or censure as being wrong
Y. Grief over someone's death

Cry Beloved Vocabulary Matching 4 Answer Key

J - 1. VERANDAHS
A - 2. COMPELLED
T - 3. MUNICIPALITY
S - 4. INELUCTABLE
B - 5. ARRAY
P - 6. HINDRANCE
F - 7. MOULD
U - 8. VICIOUSLY
C - 9. ASTRAY
R - 10. VACILLATE
X - 11. CULPABLE
H - 12. CUNNING
K - 13. CONVEY
E - 14. LINGO
V - 15. LORRY
D - 16. ACCOMPLICES
Q - 17. SYMPOSIUM
L - 18. BOYCOTT
W - 19. INCORRUPTIBLE
N - 20. DOGGEDLY
G - 21. TREMULOUS
I - 22. EXPOSITION
O - 23. FIDELITY
Y - 24. BEREAVEMENT
M - 25. SUMMON

A. Forced to action
B. Display
C. Away from the correct path or direction
D. Those who aid a lawbreaker in a criminal act
E. Language
F. General shape or form
G. Marked by trembling, quivering, or shaking
H. Subtle; deceitful
I. A statement or rhetorical discourse intended to give information about or explain difficult material
J. A porch or balcony, usually roofed, often partly enclosed, extending along the outside of a building
K. To communicate or make known
L. To abstain from using, buying, or dealing with as a form of protest
M. Gather together
N. Stubbornly persevering; tenaciously
O. Faithfulness to obligations, or duties
P. An impediment; something that gets in the way
Q. A meeting or conference for discussion of a topic
R. To swing indecisively from one course of action or opinion to another
S. Not to be avoided or escaped; inevitable
T. A political unit, such as a city or town, incorporated for local self-government
U. Aggressively; savagely
V. A motor truck
W. Incapable of being swayed to do anything immoral, illegal, or unethical
X. Deserving of blame or censure as being wrong
Y. Grief over someone's death

Cry Beloved Vocabulary Magic Squares 1

Match the definition with the vocabulary word. Put your answers in the magic squares below. When your answers are correct, all columns and rows will add to the same number.

A. HINDRANCE
B. NEGROPHILE
C. MOULD
D. INEVITABLE
E. VACILLATE
F. LORRY
G. WARDER
H. BRACKEN
I. ASTRAY
J. KLOOF
K. DOGGEDLY
L. FIDELITY
M. CLEAVE
N. CUNNING
O. PARSON
P. ASTONISHED

1. One friendly to Negros and their interests
2. A guard
3. Stubbornly persevering; tenaciously
4. Subtle; deceitful
5. To split with a sharp instrument
6. Faithfulness to obligations, or duties
7. A widespread, often weedy fern
8. An impediment; something that gets in the way
9. To fill with sudden wonder or amazement
10. Away from the correct path or direction
11. To swing indecisively from one course of action or opinion to another
12. Impossible to avoid or prevent
13. General shape or form
14. A motor truck
15. Ravine
16. A member of the clergy, especially a Protestant minister

A=	B=	C=	D=
E=	F=	G=	H=
I=	J=	K=	L=
M=	N=	O=	P=

Cry Beloved Vocabulary Magic Squares 1 Answer Key

Match the definition with the vocabulary word. Put your answers in the magic squares below. When your answers are correct, all columns and rows will add to the same number.

A. HINDRANCE
B. NEGROPHILE
C. MOULD
D. INEVITABLE
E. VACILLATE
F. LORRY
G. WARDER
H. BRACKEN
I. ASTRAY
J. KLOOF
K. DOGGEDLY
L. FIDELITY
M. CLEAVE
N. CUNNING
O. PARSON
P. ASTONISHED

1. One friendly to Negros and their interests
2. A guard
3. Stubbornly persevering; tenaciously
4. Subtle; deceitful
5. To split with a sharp instrument
6. Faithfulness to obligations, or duties
7. A widespread, often weedy fern
8. An impediment; something that gets in the way
9. To fill with sudden wonder or amazement
10. Away from the correct path or direction
11. To swing indecisively from one course of action or opinion to another
12. Impossible to avoid or prevent
13. General shape or form
14. A motor truck
15. Ravine
16. A member of the clergy, especially a Protestant minister

A=8	B=1	C=13	D=12
E=11	F=14	G=2	H=7
I=10	J=15	K=3	L=6
M=5	N=4	O=16	P=9

Cry Beloved Vocabulary Magic Squares 2

Match the definition with the vocabulary word. Put your answers in the magic squares below. When your answers are correct, all columns and rows will add to the same number.

A. PILGRIMAGE
B. EXPOSITION
C. CULPABLE
D. DELUSION
E. ENRAPT
F. OBSCURE
G. PROVISIONALLY
H. CONGENIAL
I. ACCOMPLICES
J. INCORRUPTIBLE
K. REPENT
L. SUMMON
M. INEVITABLE
N. CUNNING
O. LORRY
P. VAGABONDS

1. Deserving of blame or censure as being wrong
2. Incapable of being swayed to do anything immoral, illegal, or unethical
3. Hidden; not clearly understood
4. A motor truck
5. People without a permanent home who move from place to place
6. To fill with rapture or delight
7. Those who aid a lawbreaker in a criminal act
8. A false belief or opinion
9. Impossible to avoid or prevent
10. Suited to one's needs or nature; agreeable
11. Gather together
12. A long journey or search
13. A statement or rhetorical discourse intended to give information about or explain difficult material
14. To feel such regret for past conduct as to change one's mind regarding it
15. Temporarily
16. Subtle; deceitful

A=	B=	C=	D=
E=	F=	G=	H=
I=	J=	K=	L=
M=	N=	O=	P=

Cry Beloved Vocabulary Magic Squares 2 Answer Key

Match the definition with the vocabulary word. Put your answers in the magic squares below. When your answers are correct, all columns and rows will add to the same number.

A. PILGRIMAGE
B. EXPOSITION
C. CULPABLE
D. DELUSION
E. ENRAPT
F. OBSCURE
G. PROVISIONALLY
H. CONGENIAL
I. ACCOMPLICES
J. INCORRUPTIBLE
K. REPENT
L. SUMMON
M. INEVITABLE
N. CUNNING
O. LORRY
P. VAGABONDS

1. Deserving of blame or censure as being wrong
2. Incapable of being swayed to do anything immoral, illegal, or unethical
3. Hidden; not clearly understood
4. A motor truck
5. People without a permanent home who move from place to place
6. To fill with rapture or delight
7. Those who aid a lawbreaker in a criminal act
8. A false belief or opinion
9. Impossible to avoid or prevent
10. Suited to one's needs or nature; agreeable
11. Gather together
12. A long journey or search
13. A statement or rhetorical discourse intended to give information about or explain difficult material
14. To feel such regret for past conduct as to change one's mind regarding it
15. Temporarily
16. Subtle; deceitful

A=12	B=13	C=1	D=8
E=6	F=3	G=15	H=10
I=7	J=2	K=14	L=11
M=9	N=16	O=4	P=5

Cry Beloved Vocabulary Magic Squares 3

Match the definition with the vocabulary word. Put your answers in the magic squares below. When your answers are correct, all columns and rows will add to the same number.

A. REPROACHFULLY
B. BOYCOTT
C. INEVITABLE
D. VACILLATE
E. DELUSION
F. SUBSIDIES
G. KLOOF
H. REPENT
I. CORRUPTED
J. TREMULOUS
K. ENRAPT
L. COMPELLED
M. TRAVAIL
N. ASTRAY
O. VICIOUSLY
P. MENACE

1. To feel such regret for past conduct as to change one's mind regarding it
2. Work; painful effort; toil
3. To abstain from using, buying, or dealing with as a form of protest
4. To fill with rapture or delight
5. Marked by trembling, quivering, or shaking
6. Impossible to avoid or prevent
7. A possible danger; a threat
8. A false belief or opinion
9. Aggressively; savagely
10. Monetary assistance granted by a government
11. Marked by immorality and perversion
12. To swing indecisively from one course of action or opinion to another
13. Expressing blame
14. Forced to action
15. Ravine
16. Away from the correct path or direction

A=	B=	C=	D=
E=	F=	G=	H=
I=	J=	K=	L=
M=	N=	O=	P=

Cry Beloved Vocabulary Magic Squares 3 Answer Key

Match the definition with the vocabulary word. Put your answers in the magic squares below. When your answers are correct, all columns and rows will add to the same number.

A. REPROACHFULLY
B. BOYCOTT
C. INEVITABLE
D. VACILLATE
E. DELUSION
F. SUBSIDIES
G. KLOOF
H. REPENT
I. CORRUPTED
J. TREMULOUS
K. ENRAPT
L. COMPELLED
M. TRAVAIL
N. ASTRAY
O. VICIOUSLY
P. MENACE

1. To feel such regret for past conduct as to change one's mind regarding it
2. Work; painful effort; toil
3. To abstain from using, buying, or dealing with as a form of protest
4. To fill with rapture or delight
5. Marked by trembling, quivering, or shaking
6. Impossible to avoid or prevent
7. A possible danger; a threat
8. A false belief or opinion
9. Aggressively; savagely
10. Monetary assistance granted by a government
11. Marked by immorality and perversion
12. To swing indecisively from one course of action or opinion to another
13. Expressing blame
14. Forced to action
15. Ravine
16. Away from the correct path or direction

A=13	B=3	C=6	D=12
E=8	F=10	G=15	H=1
I=11	J=5	K=4	L=14
M=2	N=16	O=9	P=7

Cry Beloved Vocabulary Magic Squares 4

Match the definition with the vocabulary word. Put your answers in the magic squares below. When your answers are correct, all columns and rows will add to the same number.

A. DELUSION
B. KLOOF
C. MOULD
D. VAGABONDS
E. ACCOMPLICES
F. VICIOUSLY
G. GRATIFY
H. EXPLOITATION
I. SYMPOSIUM
J. TREMULOUS
K. VERANDAHS
L. MENACE
M. SOMBRE
N. KRAAL
O. PRELUDE
P. TIERS

1. A false belief or opinion
2. A rural village
3. Marked by trembling, quivering, or shaking
4. Those who aid a lawbreaker in a criminal act
5. To please or satisfy
6. A possible danger; a threat
7. One of a series of rows placed one above another
8. General shape or form
9. Introduction
10. People without a permanent home who move from place to place
11. Taking advantage of people or a situation for monetary gain
12. A porch or balcony, usually roofed, often partly enclosed, extending along the outside of a building
13. A meeting or conference for discussion of a topic
14. Aggressively; savagely
15. Ravine
16. Dark; gloomy; serious; grave

A=	B=	C=	D=
E=	F=	G=	H=
I=	J=	K=	L=
M=	N=	O=	P=

Cry Beloved Vocabulary Magic Squares 4 Answer Key

Match the definition with the vocabulary word. Put your answers in the magic squares below. When your answers are correct, all columns and rows will add to the same number.

A. DELUSION
B. KLOOF
C. MOULD
D. VAGABONDS
E. ACCOMPLICES
F. VICIOUSLY
G. GRATIFY
H. EXPLOITATION
I. SYMPOSIUM
J. TREMULOUS
K. VERANDAHS
L. MENACE
M. SOMBRE
N. KRAAL
O. PRELUDE
P. TIERS

1. A false belief or opinion
2. A rural village
3. Marked by trembling, quivering, or shaking
4. Those who aid a lawbreaker in a criminal act
5. To please or satisfy
6. A possible danger; a threat
7. One of a series of rows placed one above another
8. General shape or form
9. Introduction
10. People without a permanent home who move from place to place
11. Taking advantage of people or a situation for monetary gain
12. A porch or balcony, usually roofed, often partly enclosed, extending along the outside of a building
13. A meeting or conference for discussion of a topic
14. Aggressively; savagely
15. Ravine
16. Dark; gloomy; serious; grave

A=1	B=15	C=8	D=10
E=4	F=14	G=5	H=11
I=13	J=3	K=12	L=6
M=16	N=2	O=9	P=7

Cry Beloved Vocabulary Word Search 1

Words are placed backwards, forward, diagonally, up and down. Clues listed below can help you find the words. Circle the hidden vocabulary words in the maze.

A	V	E	R	A	N	D	A	H	S	D	N	M	A	B	I	D	E	C	W
B	P	C	D	E	D	N	E	M	A	F	E	L	I	N	G	O	V	Y	Z
A	X	N	A	Y	P	S	R	M	S	U	L	L	E	N	L	Y	F	I	G
T	K	L	C	O	R	R	U	P	T	E	D	E	L	U	S	I	O	N	M
I	A	L	C	J	N	I	C	M	C	I	I	M	N	K	T	F	I	E	N
N	S	T	O	L	S	L	S	W	M	R	E	E	X	A	E	N	C	L	S
G	T	R	M	O	G	D	B	R	E	O	N	R	R	V	N	P	O	U	K
D	R	E	P	R	F	Q	O	V	J	D	N	G	S	U	R	R	N	C	V
E	A	M	L	R	Y	V	E	G	U	B	B	C	C	J	A	E	G	T	Q
H	Y	U	I	Y	S	R	G	R	G	Y	L	R	J	Y	P	L	E	A	V
S	D	L	C	U	L	P	A	B	L	E	M	D	A	O	T	U	N	B	D
I	U	O	E	N	V	B	C	S	A	W	D	R	B	C	F	D	I	L	Y
N	B	U	S	D	L	N	U	V	A	D	R	L	Z	S	K	E	A	E	H
O	I	S	Q	E	O	O	E	R	R	A	I	D	Y	Q	O	E	L	P	S
T	O	G	L	S	I	H	D	Z	K	G	L	X	B	G	L	M	N	Z	D
S	U	V	R	C	P	E	Z	X	I	U	T	T	O	C	Y	O	B	R	G
A	S	A	I	Q	R	H	J	N	O	R	E	P	E	N	T	X	Z	R	T
L	P	V	C	P	G	K	G	M	P	E	R	M	I	S	S	I	B	L	E

A false belief or opinion (8)
A guard (6)
A meeting or conference for discussion of a topic (9)
A member of the clergy, especially a Protestant minister (6)
A motor truck (5)
A porch or balcony, usually roofed, often partly enclosed, extending along the outside of a building
A rural village (5)
A small, secluded, wooded valley (4)
A widespread, often weedy fern (7)
Aggressively; savagely (9)
Away from the correct path or direction (6)
Dark; gloomy; serious; grave (6)
Daydream (7)
Deserving of blame or censure as being wrong (8)
Display (5)
Doubtful (7)
Gather together (6)
General shape or form (5)
Hidden; not clearly understood (7)
Improved (7)
Introduction (7)
Language (5)

Lessening (7)
Marked by immorality and perversion (9)
Marked by trembling, quivering, or shaking (9)
Not to be avoided or escaped; inevitable (11)
One of a series of rows placed one above another (5)
Permitted; allowable (11)
Ravine (5)
Showing a brooding ill humor (8)
Stubbornly persevering; tenaciously (8)
Subtle; deceitful (7)
Suited to one's needs or nature; agreeable (9)
Those who aid a lawbreaker in a criminal act (11)
To abstain from using, buying, or dealing with as a form of protest (7)
To feel such regret for past conduct as to change one's mind regarding it (6)
To fill with rapture or delight (6)
To fill with sudden wonder or amazement (10)
To please or satisfy (7)
To remain in place (5)
To split with a sharp instrument (6)
Unbearable (11)
Willing to do a service or favor for (8)

Cry Beloved Vocabulary Word Search 1 Answer Key

Words are placed backwards, forward, diagonally, up and down. Clues listed below can help you find the words. Circle the hidden vocabulary words in the maze.

- A false belief or opinion (8)
- A guard (6)
- A meeting or conference for discussion of a topic (9)
- A member of the clergy, especially a Protestant minister (6)
- A motor truck (5)
- A porch or balcony, usually roofed, often partly enclosed, extending along the outside of a building
- A rural village (5)
- A small, secluded, wooded valley (4)
- A widespread, often weedy fern (7)
- Aggressively; savagely (9)
- Away from the correct path or direction (6)
- Dark; gloomy; serious; grave (6)
- Daydream (7)
- Deserving of blame or censure as being wrong (8)
- Display (5)
- Doubtful (7)
- Gather together (6)
- General shape or form (5)
- Hidden; not clearly understood (7)
- Improved (7)
- Introduction (7)
- Language (5)
- Lessening (7)
- Marked by immorality and perversion (9)
- Marked by trembling, quivering, or shaking (9)
- Not to be avoided or escaped; inevitable (11)
- One of a series of rows placed one above another (5)
- Permitted; allowable (11)
- Ravine (5)
- Showing a brooding ill humor (8)
- Stubbornly persevering; tenaciously (8)
- Subtle; deceitful (7)
- Suited to one's needs or nature; agreeable (9)
- Those who aid a lawbreaker in a criminal act (11)
- To abstain from using, buying, or dealing with as a form of protest (7)
- To feel such regret for past conduct as to change one's mind regarding it (6)
- To fill with rapture or delight (6)
- To fill with sudden wonder or amazement (10)
- To please or satisfy (7)
- To remain in place (5)
- To split with a sharp instrument (6)
- Unbearable (11)
- Willing to do a service or favor for (8)

Cry Beloved Vocabulary Word Search 2

Words are placed backwards, forward, diagonally, up and down. Clues listed below can help you find the words. Circle the hidden vocabulary words in the maze.

```
A S T R A Y A R R A C O M P E L L E D W
V H B N M B K X Y T W D C I T B I L K T
A I N E E T I Z R G E F O L A O A B R B
G N Q K N G N D F X D N B G L Y V I A W
A D W C D O G G E D L Y L R L C A T A B
B R I A E V K L N B P D I I I O R P L T
O A M R D F P T E C R E G M C T T U E J
N N W B R R A W K Q Q L I A A T M R L J
D C A J E I I B Z R S U N G V V S R B J
S E R P N L T J A O B S G E E U M O A W
P W D G D K J A M T Y I C R M J O C R K
L A E E W N G B T X I O A M Q Y U N U E
E I R E V E R G Y E V N O C X Y L I D D
T S U S F E A P L V D N G S R I D U N D
I C C M O T T T C A H D M R N G L P E Y
E A S T O N I S H E D E O G R E P E N T
R F B X L R F S P L H L O P R S G F U J
S J O P K H Y W G C G L T P A R N E W J
```

A false belief or opinion (8)
A guard (6)
A long journey or search (10)
A member of the clergy, especially a Protestant minister (6)
A motor truck (5)
A porch or balcony, usually roofed, often partly enclosed, extending along the outside of a building
A rural village (5)
A small, secluded, wooded valley (4)
A widespread, often weedy fern (7)
An impediment; something that gets in the way (9)
Annoy; bother (8)
Away from the correct path or direction (6)
Confused or troubled with uncertainty or doubt (9)
Confuses or befuddles (9)
Dark; gloomy; serious; grave (6)
Daydream (7)
Display (5)
Forced to action (9)
Gather together (6)
General shape or form (5)
Hidden; not clearly understood (7)
Improved (7)
Incapable of being swayed to do anything immoral, illegal, or unethical (13)

Introduction (7)
Language (5)
Lessening (7)
One of a series of rows placed one above another (5)
People without a permanent home who move from place to place (9)
Ravine (5)
Stubbornly persevering; tenaciously (8)
To abstain from using, buying, or dealing with as a form of protest (7)
To communicate or make known (6)
To feel such regret for past conduct as to change one's mind regarding it (6)
To fill with rapture or delight (6)
To fill with sudden wonder or amazement (10)
To please or satisfy (7)
To remain in place (5)
To split with a sharp instrument (6)
To swing indecisively from one course of action or opinion to another (9)
Unbearable (11)
Willing to do a service or favor for (8)
Work; painful effort; toil (7)

Cry Beloved Vocabulary Word Search 2 Answer Key

Words are placed backwards, forward, diagonally, up and down. Clues listed below can help you find the words. Circle the hidden vocabulary words in the maze.

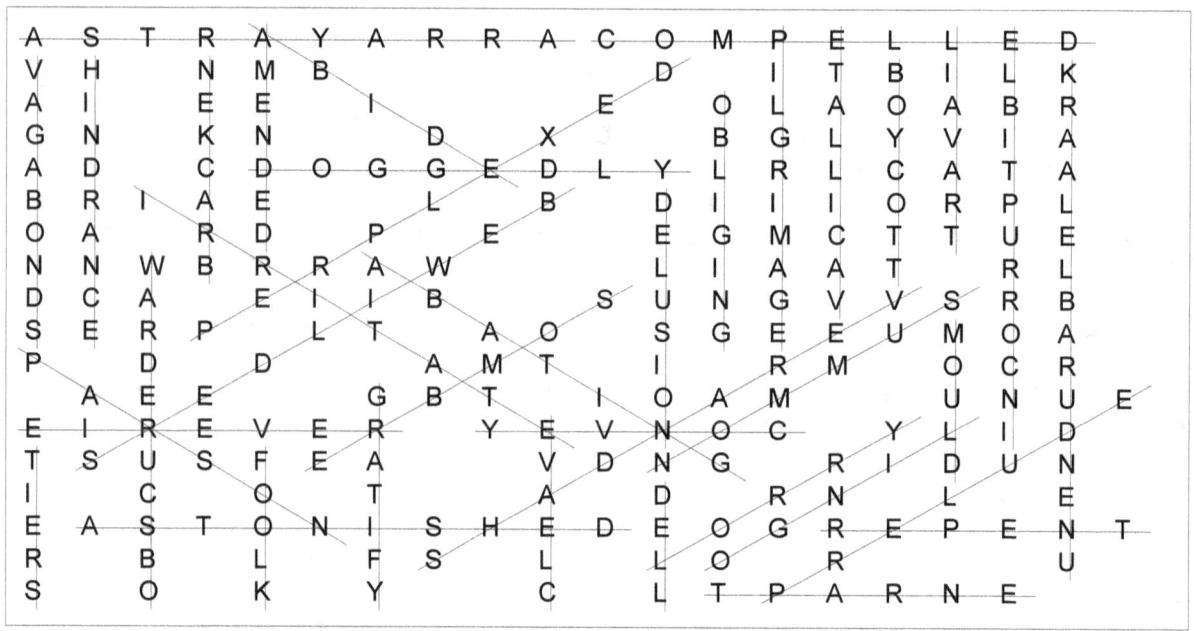

A false belief or opinion (8)
A guard (6)
A long journey or search (10)
A member of the clergy, especially a Protestant minister (6)
A motor truck (5)
A porch or balcony, usually roofed, often partly enclosed, extending along the outside of a building
A rural village (5)
A small, secluded, wooded valley (4)
A widespread, often weedy fern (7)
An impediment; something that gets in the way (9)
Annoy; bother (8)
Away from the correct path or direction (6)
Confused or troubled with uncertainty or doubt (9)
Confuses or befuddles (9)
Dark; gloomy; serious; grave (6)
Daydream (7)
Display (5)
Forced to action (9)
Gather together (6)
General shape or form (5)
Hidden; not clearly understood (7)
Improved (7)
Incapable of being swayed to do anything immoral, illegal, or unethical (13)

Introduction (7)
Language (5)
Lessening (7)
One of a series of rows placed one above another (5)
People without a permanent home who move from place to place (9)
Ravine (5)
Stubbornly persevering; tenaciously (8)
To abstain from using, buying, or dealing with as a form of protest (7)
To communicate or make known (6)
To feel such regret for past conduct as to change one's mind regarding it (6)
To fill with rapture or delight (6)
To fill with sudden wonder or amazement (10)
To please or satisfy (7)
To remain in place (5)
To split with a sharp instrument (6)
To swing indecisively from one course of action or opinion to another (9)
Unbearable (11)
Willing to do a service or favor for (8)
Work; painful effort; toil (7)

Cry Beloved Vocabulary Word Search 3

Words are placed backwards, forward, diagonally, up and down. Words listed below are included in the maze. Circle the hidden vocabulary words in the maze.

```
S U L L E N L Y S E E D I B A M D D Y Q
U A B A T I N G N L L R A G Z S B A Z N
M E I R E V E R B B B V M N K P R D Y C
M K L O O F A A F I A F E I T R A U L W
O F X F S P T Y W S P G N N A B C B L G
N J D G T I X D B S L E D N C O K I U M
K L K E V X E K D I U L E U E Y E O F B
V G V E S L N E D M C B D C C C N U H Y
F M N Q U O L V C R Z A U O N O W S C T
Y I Y S B L L P Z E Z R L N A T N N A R
E B I C E T A A G P S U E G R T N O O I
V O K P W R S B T O K D R E D I V S R S
N D M Y I J P N M I H N P N N E J R P S
O O G A L K I B H M O E T I I R E A E T
C W A R D E R V E R A N D A H S E P R P
M L H T E E A A X G E U Z L O C N A U G
O Y E S R F T Q A P Z K L L A J V W C X
U B B A S N I Q E L D L U N H A J D S P
L D P P V K O R W T E T E L I N G O B Z
D P X K L E N Y Y D E M G L R Y R R O L
```

ABATING	CONGENIAL	IRRESOLUTE	REPENT
ABIDE	CONVEY	KLOOF	REPROACHFULLY
AMENDED	CULPABLE	KRAAL	REVERIE
ARRAY	CUNNING	LINGO	SOMBRE
ASPIRATION	DELL	LORRY	SULLENLY
ASTRAY	DELUSION	MENACE	SUMMON
BEWILDERS	DESOLATION	MOULD	TIERS
BOYCOTT	DUBIOUS	OBSCURE	TRAVAIL
BRACKEN	ENRAPT	PARSON	UNENDURABLE
CLEAVE	HINDRANCE	PERMISSIBLE	VERANDAHS
COMPELLED	INEVITABLE	PRELUDE	WARDER

Cry Beloved Vocabulary Word Search 3 Answer Key

Words are placed backwards, forward, diagonally, up and down. Words listed below are included in the maze. Circle the hidden vocabulary words in the maze.

```
S U L L E N L Y       E   E D I B A             Y
U A B A T I N G N     L   L   A G         B A
M E I R E V E R B B   B   B   M N         R D Y
M K L O O F A A       I   A   E I     R   A U L
O         P T         S   P   N N   A B   C B L
N     D   T I   D     S   L   D N   E O   K I U
        E V     E D   I   U   E E   E C   E O F
        E S L     E   M C B   D C   N O   N S H
      N   U O L       R   A   U O   C T   S N C
  Y I   S B L L     P S U L   N A   O T   N O A
  E   O P E A A   T   O D R   G R   N I   O S O
  V   M Y W S P M     M N E   E D   T E   S R R I
  N O O A I K I B     M O P   N N   E R   R R P
  O   C W A R D E R V E R A N D A H S E P E E T
  C M   L T E E A A       E U   L O C     P R U
  O U     E S R   A T   A P     L L A     A U C
  U L       A S   T I   E L     U N A     V C S
  L D         V   O R     E T E L I N G O B
              E   N     D E M   L     Y R R O L
```

ABATING	CONGENIAL	IRRESOLUTE	REPENT
ABIDE	CONVEY	KLOOF	REPROACHFULLY
AMENDED	CULPABLE	KRAAL	REVERIE
ARRAY	CUNNING	LINGO	SOMBRE
ASPIRATION	DELL	LORRY	SULLENLY
ASTRAY	DELUSION	MENACE	SUMMON
BEWILDERS	DESOLATION	MOULD	TIERS
BOYCOTT	DUBIOUS	OBSCURE	TRAVAIL
BRACKEN	ENRAPT	PARSON	UNENDURABLE
CLEAVE	HINDRANCE	PERMISSIBLE	VERANDAHS
COMPELLED	INEVITABLE	PRELUDE	WARDER

Cry Beloved Vocabulary Word Search 4

Words are placed backwards, forward, diagonally, up and down. Words listed below are included in the maze. Circle the hidden vocabulary words in the maze.

```
O D O G G E D L Y T I L A P I C I N U M
B F P C R K C Z H M D F S B A A R D Y T
L K I O A K U W D M S I T I A R B C T R
I V L N T C L E A V E D R R W T S I B S
G P G V I D P O P J G E A R A S I O D W
I T R E F V A H O N N L Y I R O D N N E
N D I Y Y S B J F F X I Z T D M G G G R
G E M A G L L A A R K T C A E B T K S F
S T A R V K E N H W L Y V T R R Y A T E
S P G R R A B O Y C O T T E K E S Z N Y
E U E A E C A N E M W B M N T X R I F
C R X N P L K I S X E G E T O J A J A M
I R H Z E I C L L D C C W N S P C M R Q
L O E T N A W J U L S M I B T U O D T M
P C Y V T V X L R H A S L F S U M J S F
M W C W E A E H K T H T D R L L L M N L
O B S C U R E A M E N D E D L I N G O L
C W R L P T I S D S S I R E N F Y R C N
C O M P E L L E D V T H S L R K R S W K
A P E R P L E X E D Y S V L Y Y P R F Z
```

ABATING	CLEAVE	FIDELITY	MUNICIPALITY	SOMBRE
ABIDE	COMPELLED	GRATIFY	OBLIGING	SUMMON
ACCOMPLICES	CONSTRAINT	IRRITATE	OBSCURE	TIERS
AMENDED	CONVEY	KLOOF	PARSON	TRAVAIL
ARRAY	CORRUPTED	KRAAL	PERPLEXED	VACILLATE
ASTONISHED	CULPABLE	LINGO	PILGRIMAGE	WARDER
ASTRAY	DELL	LORRY	PRELUDE	
BEWILDERS	DOGGEDLY	MENACE	REPENT	
BOYCOTT	ENRAPT	MOULD	REVERIE	

Cry Beloved Vocabulary Word Search 4 Answer Key

Words are placed backwards, forward, diagonally, up and down. Words listed below are included in the maze. Circle the hidden vocabulary words in the maze.

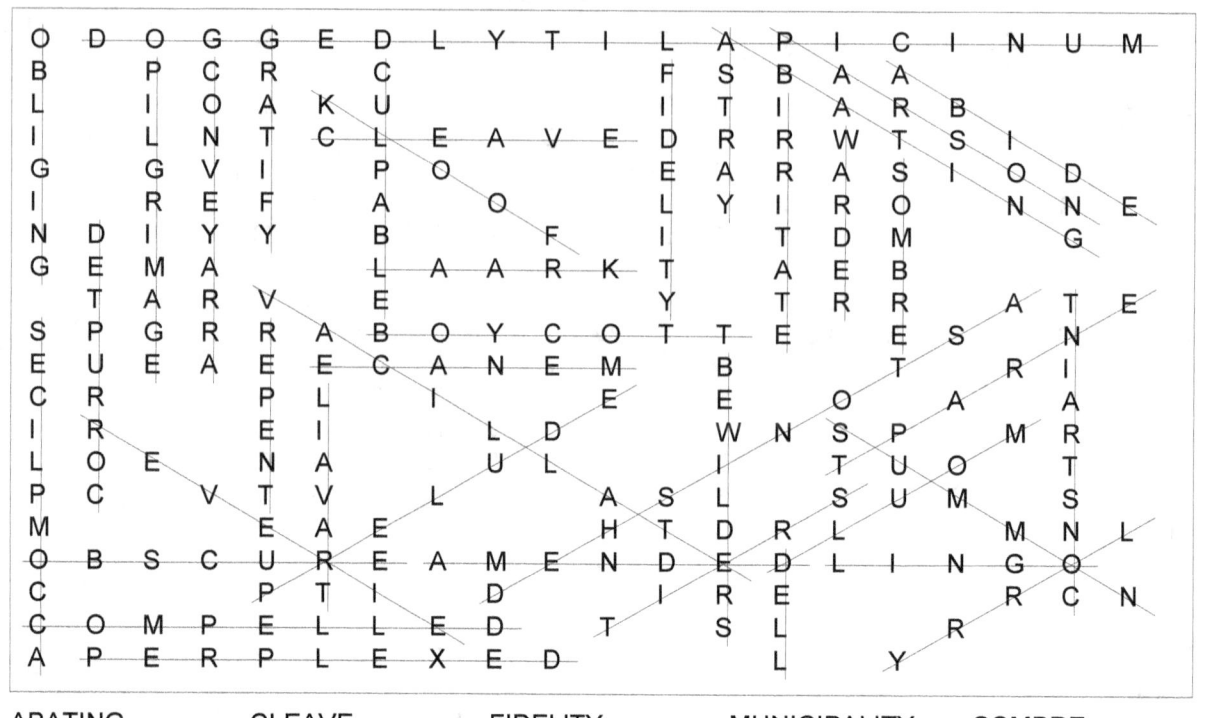

ABATING	CLEAVE	FIDELITY	MUNICIPALITY	SOMBRE
ABIDE	COMPELLED	GRATIFY	OBLIGING	SUMMON
ACCOMPLICES	CONSTRAINT	IRRITATE	OBSCURE	TIERS
AMENDED	CONVEY	KLOOF	PARSON	TRAVAIL
ARRAY	CORRUPTED	KRAAL	PERPLEXED	VACILLATE
ASTONISHED	CULPABLE	LINGO	PILGRIMAGE	WARDER
ASTRAY	DELL	LORRY	PRELUDE	
BEWILDERS	DOGGEDLY	MENACE	REPENT	
BOYCOTT	ENRAPT	MOULD	REVERIE	

Cry Beloved Vocabulary Crossword 1

Across
1. People without a permanent home who move from place to place
6. A statement or rhetorical discourse intended to give information about or explain difficult material
10. General shape or form
12. A member of the clergy, especially a Protestant minister
14. To remain in place
16. Display
17. A small, secluded, wooded valley
20. A possible danger; a threat
21. Suited to one's needs or nature; agreeable
22. A political unit, such as a city or town, incorporated for local self-government

Down
2. Away from the correct path or direction
3. Dark; gloomy; serious; grave
4. One friendly to Negros and their interests
5. Subtle; deceitful
7. A long journey or search
8. Gather together
9. Willing to do a service or favor for
11. A false belief or opinion
13. Daydream
14. A strong desire for high achievement; ambition
15. Work; painful effort; toil
18. Language
19. To feel such regret for past conduct as to change one's mind regarding it

Cry Beloved Vocabulary Crossword 1 Answer Key

			1 V	A	G	2 A	B	O	N	D	3 S			
		4 N				S					O		5 C	
6 E	7 X	8 P	O	S	I	T	I	O	N		10 M	O	U	L	11 D
G		I		U		R		B			B		N		E
R		L		M		A		L			R		N		L
O		G		M		Y		I			E		I		U
12 P	A	R	S	O	N			G		13 R			N		S
H		I		N		14 A	B	I	D	E			G		I
I		M				S		N		V		15 T			O
L		A				P		G		E		R			N
E		G				I			16 A	R	R	A	Y		
	17 D	18 E	L	L		R			I		V		19 R		
		I		A				20 M	E	N	A	C	E		
		N		T					I				P		
21 C	O	N	G	E	N	I	A	L			L		E		
				O		O					N				
			22 M	U	N	I	C	I	P	A	L	I	T	Y	

Across
1. People without a permanent home who move from place to place
6. A statement or rhetorical discourse intended to give information about or explain difficult material
10. General shape or form
12. A member of the clergy, especially a Protestant minister
14. To remain in place
16. Display
17. A small, secluded, wooded valley
20. A possible danger; a threat
21. Suited to one's needs or nature; agreeable
22. A political unit, such as a city or town, incorporated for local self-government

Down
2. Away from the correct path or direction
3. Dark; gloomy; serious; grave
4. One friendly to Negros and their interests
5. Subtle; deceitful
7. A long journey or search
8. Gather together
9. Willing to do a service or favor for
11. A false belief or opinion
13. Daydream
14. A strong desire for high achievement; ambition
15. Work; painful effort; toil
18. Language
19. To feel such regret for past conduct as to change one's mind regarding it

Cry Beloved Vocabulary Crossword 2

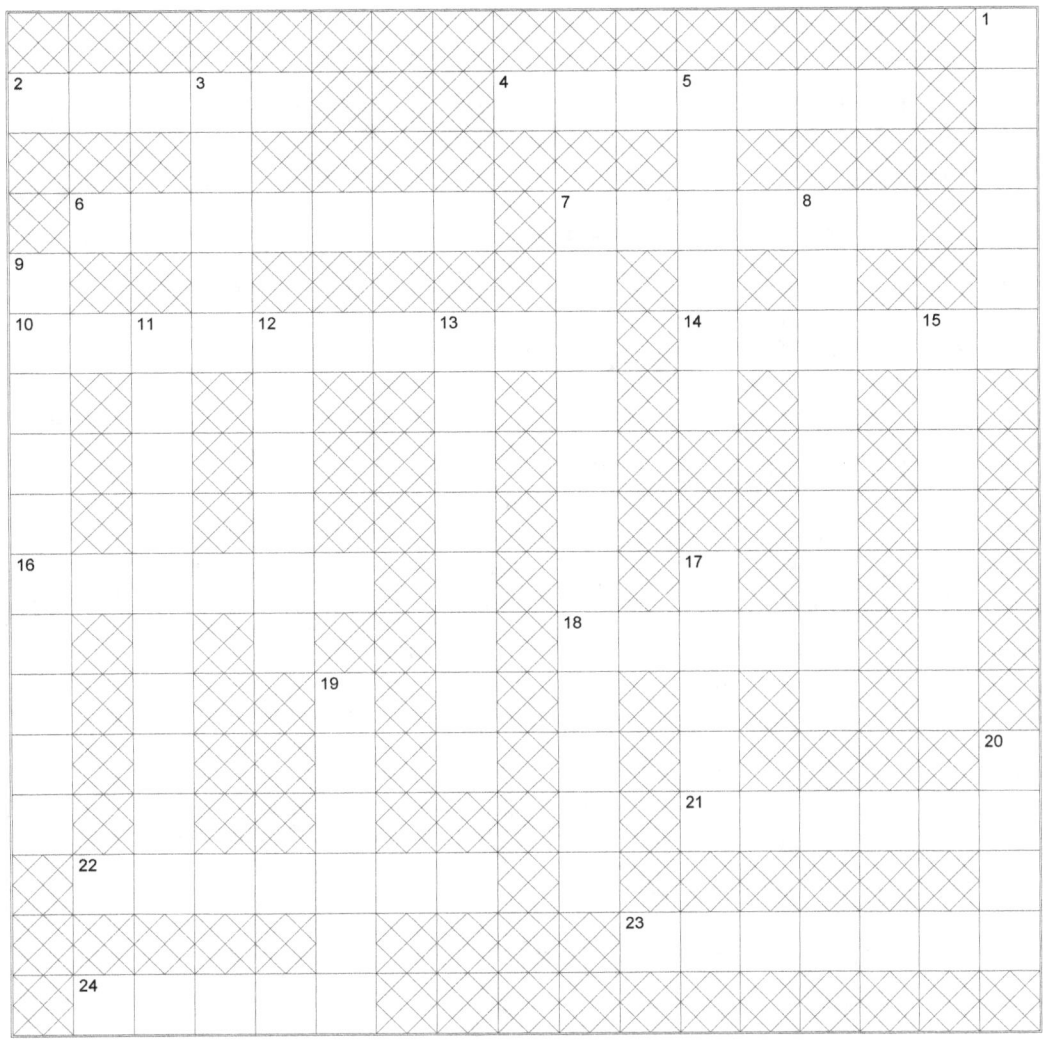

Across
2. General shape or form
4. A widespread, often weedy fern
6. Subtle; deceitful
7. A possible danger; a threat
10. A statement or rhetorical discourse intended to give information about or explain difficult material
14. To fill with rapture or delight
16. A member of the clergy, especially a Protestant minister
18. To remain in place
21. Dark; gloomy; serious; grave
22. Daydream
23. Work; painful effort; toil
24. Display

Down
1. To feel such regret for past conduct as to change one's mind regarding it
3. Language
5. To communicate or make known
7. A political unit, such as a city or town, incorporated for local self-government
8. Marked by immorality and perversion
9. One friendly to Negros and their interests
11. A long journey or search
12. Gather together
13. Annoy; bother
15. Introduction
17. One of a series of rows placed one above another
19. Away from the correct path or direction
20. A small, secluded, wooded valley

Cry Beloved Vocabulary Crossword 2 Answer Key

		2 M	O	3 U L I G	D		4 B	R	5 C O	K	E	N		1 R E P E N
		6 C	U	N	N	I	N G	7 M	E	N	A	8 C E	E	
		9 N		G				U		V		O		N
		10 E	11 X P I L G A I M A G	12 S U M M	I	13 T I R R I	O	N	14 E Y		N	15 R A P R R E L U D E	T
		16 P A H I L E		R S I N	O	N T A	18 A B L I T Y	B	I R E R S	D	E D D	20 D E L
			22 R	E	V	E	R	I	E	21 S T	O	M	B	R E L
			24 A	R	R	A	Y			23 T	R	A	V	I L

Across
2. General shape or form
4. A widespread, often weedy fern
6. Subtle; deceitful
7. A possible danger; a threat
10. A statement or rhetorical discourse intended to give information about or explain difficult material
14. To fill with rapture or delight
16. A member of the clergy, especially a Protestant minister
18. To remain in place
21. Dark; gloomy; serious; grave
22. Daydream
23. Work; painful effort; toil
24. Display

Down
1. To feel such regret for past conduct as to change one's mind regarding it
3. Language
5. To communicate or make known
7. A political unit, such as a city or town, incorporated for local self-government
8. Marked by immorality and perversion
9. One friendly to Negros and their interests
11. A long journey or search
12. Gather together
13. Annoy; bother
15. Introduction
17. One of a series of rows placed one above another
19. Away from the correct path or direction
20. A small, secluded, wooded valley

Cry Beloved Vocabulary Crossword 3

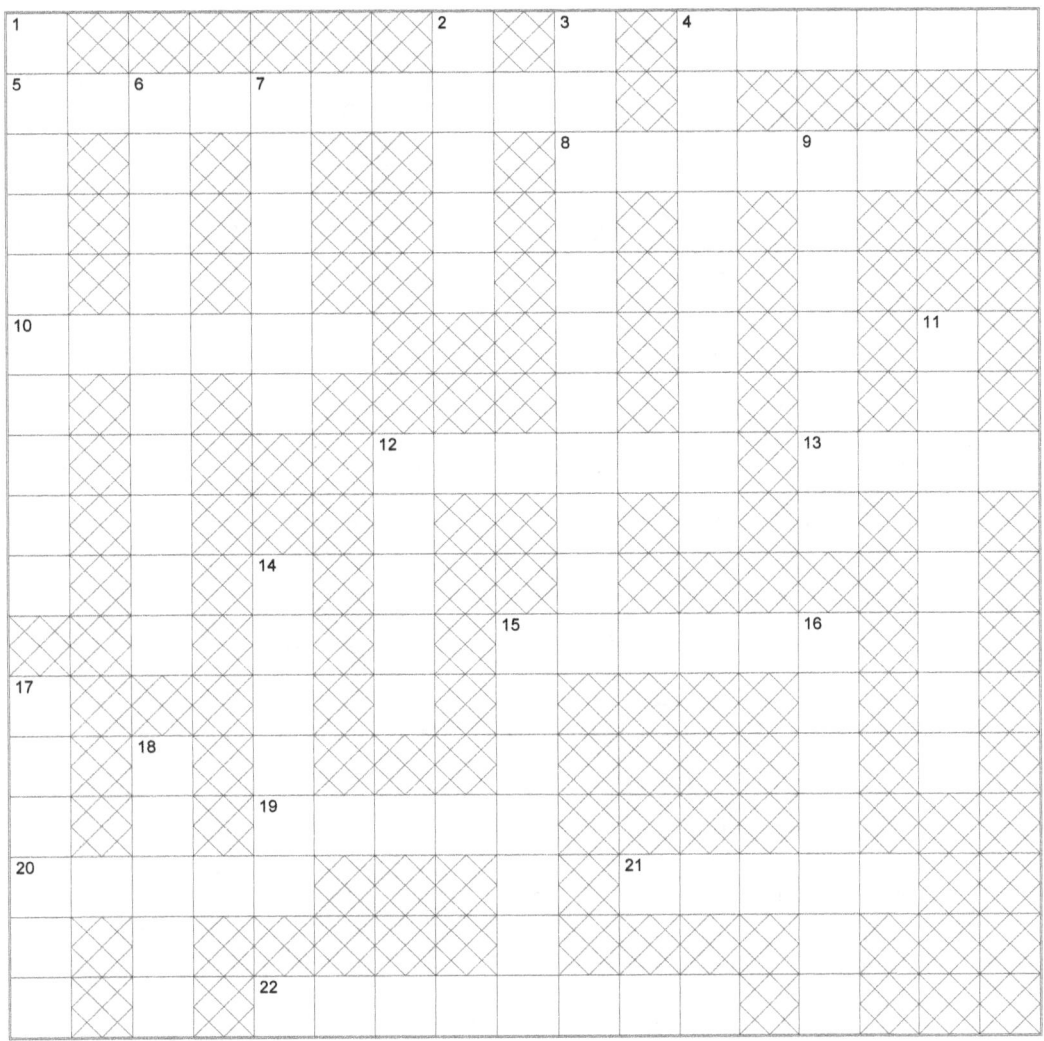

Across
4. To communicate or make known
5. A statement or rhetorical discourse intended to give information about or explain difficult material
8. To fill with rapture or delight
10. A member of the clergy, especially a Protestant minister
12. A possible danger; a threat
13. A small, secluded, wooded valley
15. To feel such regret for past conduct as to change one's mind regarding it
19. To remain in place
20. Display
21. A rural village
22. Stubbornly persevering; tenaciously

Down
1. One friendly to Negros and their interests
2. Language
3. Unbearable
4. Marked by immorality and perversion
6. A long journey or search
7. Gather together
9. Introduction
11. A false belief or opinion
12. General shape or form
14. Away from the correct path or direction
15. Daydream
16. Work; painful effort; toil
17. To split with a sharp instrument
18. A motor truck

Cry Beloved Vocabulary Crossword 3 Answer Key

	1	2	3	4			
	N		L	U	C	O	N	V	E	Y
5	E	6 X	7 P	O	S	I	T	I	O	N	O
	G		I		U		N		8 E	N	R	A	9 P	T
	R		L		M		N		G		N		R		R
	O		G		M				O		D		U		E
10 P	A	R	S	O	N				U		P		L		11 D
	H		I		N				R		T		U		E
	I		M				12 M	E	N	A	C	E	13 D	E	L	L
	L		A				O		B		D		E		U
	E		G		14 A	U	L		L				E		S
			E		S			15 R	E	P	E	N	16 T		I
17 C				T		D		E					R		O
	L		18 L		R			V					A		N
	E		O		19 A	B	I	D	E				V		
20 A	R	R	A	Y				R		21 K	R	A	A	L	
	V		R					I					I		
	E		22 Y		D	O	G	G	E	D	L	Y		L	

Across

4. To communicate or make known
5. A statement or rhetorical discourse intended to give information about or explain difficult material
8. To fill with rapture or delight
10. A member of the clergy, especially a Protestant minister
12. A possible danger; a threat
13. A small, secluded, wooded valley
15. To feel such regret for past conduct as to change one's mind regarding it
19. To remain in place
20. Display
21. A rural village
22. Stubbornly persevering; tenaciously

Down

1. One friendly to Negros and their interests
2. Language
3. Unbearable
4. Marked by immorality and perversion
6. A long journey or search
7. Gather together
9. Introduction
11. A false belief or opinion
12. General shape or form
14. Away from the correct path or direction
15. Daydream
16. Work; painful effort; toil
17. To split with a sharp instrument
18. A motor truck

Cry Beloved Vocabulary Crossword 4

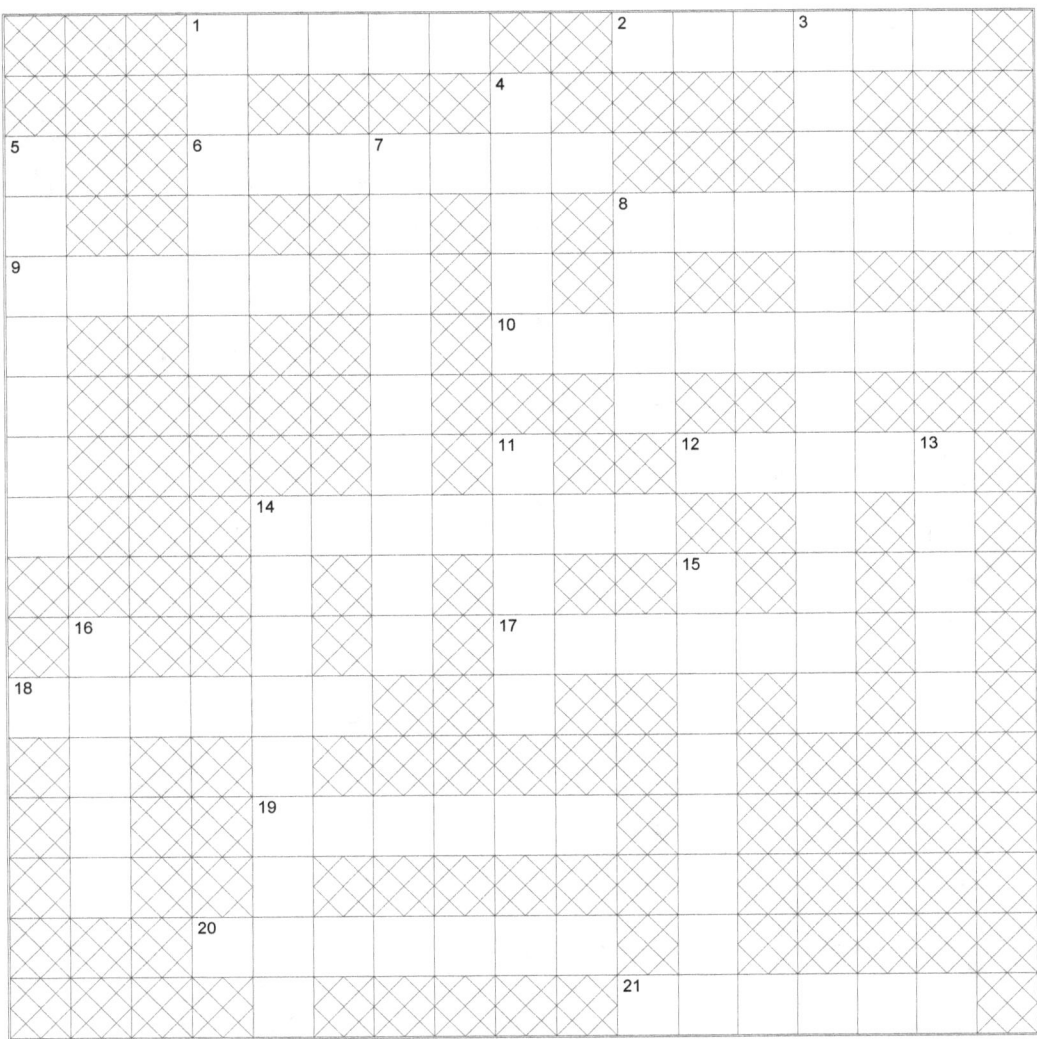

Across
1. To remain in place
2. Gather together
6. Work; painful effort; toil
8. Doubtful
9. Display
10. Willing to do a service or favor for
12. A rural village
14. Subtle; deceitful
17. To feel such regret for past conduct as to change one's mind regarding it
18. Dark; gloomy; serious; grave
19. A member of the clergy, especially a Protestant minister
20. Daydream
21. To fill with rapture or delight

Down
1. Away from the correct path or direction
3. A political unit, such as a city or town, incorporated for local self-government
4. Language
5. To please or satisfy
7. People without a permanent home who move from place to place
8. A small, secluded, wooded valley
11. One of a series of rows placed one above another
13. A motor truck
14. Marked by immorality and perversion
15. A false belief or opinion
16. General shape or form

Cry Beloved Vocabulary Crossword 4 Answer Key

		1 A	B	I	D	E		2 S	U	M	3 M	O	N	
		S				4 L					U			
5 G		6 T	R	A	7 V	A	I	L			N			
R		R			A		N		8 D	U	B	I	O	U	S
9 A	R	R	A	Y		G		G		E		C		
T		Y				A		10 O	B	L	I	G	I	N	G
I						B				L		P		
F						O		11 T		12 K	R	A	A	13 L
Y				14 C	U	N	N	I	N	G		L		O
				O		D		E		15 D		I		R
		16 M		R		S		17 R	E	P	E	N	T	R
18 S	O	M	B	R	E			S		L		Y		Y
		U		U						U				
		L		19 P	A	R	S	O	N		S			
		D		T							I			
				20 R	E	V	E	R	I	E		O		
				D						21 E	N	R	A	P	T

Across
1. To remain in place
2. Gather together
6. Work; painful effort; toil
8. Doubtful
9. Display
10. Willing to do a service or favor for
12. A rural village
14. Subtle; deceitful
17. To feel such regret for past conduct as to change one's mind regarding it
18. Dark; gloomy; serious; grave
19. A member of the clergy, especially a Protestant minister
20. Daydream
21. To fill with rapture or delight

Down
1. Away from the correct path or direction
3. A political unit, such as a city or town, incorporated for local self-government
4. Language
5. To please or satisfy
7. People without a permanent home who move from place to place
8. A small, secluded, wooded valley
11. One of a series of rows placed one above another
13. A motor truck
14. Marked by immorality and perversion
15. A false belief or opinion
16. General shape or form

Cry Beloved Vocabulary Juggle Letters 1

1. IREEREV = 1. _____
   Daydream

2. LUYELNSL = 2. _____
   Showing a brooding ill humor

3. TIAALCEVL = 3. _____
   To swing indecisively from one course of action or opinion to another

4. BCLAEUPL = 4. _____
   Deserving of blame or censure as being wrong

5. RLIPGAEGMI = 5. _____
   A long journey or search

6. GTIBAAN = 6. _____
   Lessening

7. ESRDIWELB = 7. _____
   Confuses or befuddles

8. TAENLIEIBV = 8. _____
   Impossible to avoid or prevent

9. YCVENO = 9. _____
   To communicate or make known

10. LELD = 10. _____
    A small, secluded, wooded valley

11. ROLYR = 11. _____
    A motor truck

12. OMMUNS = 12. _____
    Gather together

13. DARWER = 13. _____
    A guard

14. EMCELLPDO = 14. _____
    Forced to action

15. ORURDCTEP = 15. _____
    Marked by immorality and perversion

Cry Beloved Vocabulary Juggle Letters 1 Answer Key

1. IREEREV = 1. REVERIE
   Daydream

2. LUYELNSL = 2. SULLENLY
   Showing a brooding ill humor

3. TIAALCEVL = 3. VACILLATE
   To swing indecisively from one course of action or opinion to another

4. BCLAEUPL = 4. CULPABLE
   Deserving of blame or censure as being wrong

5. RLIPGAEGMI = 5. PILGRIMAGE
   A long journey or search

6. GTIBAAN = 6. ABATING
   Lessening

7. ESRDIWELB = 7. BEWILDERS
   Confuses or befuddles

8. TAENLIEIBV = 8. INEVITABLE
   Impossible to avoid or prevent

9. YCVENO = 9. CONVEY
   To communicate or make known

10. LELD = 10. DELL
    A small, secluded, wooded valley

11. ROLYR = 11. LORRY
    A motor truck

12. OMMUNS = 12. SUMMON
    Gather together

13. DARWER = 13. WARDER
    A guard

14. EMCELLPDO = 14. COMPELLED
    Forced to action

15. ORURDCTEP = 15. CORRUPTED
    Marked by immorality and perversion

Cry Beloved Vocabulary Juggle Letters 2

1. OEYVCN = 1. _____
   To communicate or make known

2. OYRLR = 2. _____
   A motor truck

3. TRARTIEI = 3. _____
   Annoy; bother

4. SRPAON = 4. _____
   A member of the clergy, especially a Protestant minister

5. STEUIEORRL = 5. _____
   Unsure of how to act or proceed; undecided

6. TISTACNONR = 6. _____
   Awkwardness

7. IVEEERR = 7. _____
   Daydream

8. EEDPXELPR = 8. _____
   Confused or troubled with uncertainty or doubt

9. PAITIOOLTXEN = 9. _____
   Taking advantage of people or a situation for monetary gain

10. CUIRBITOPRNLE =10. _____
    Incapable of being swayed to do anything immoral, illegal, or unethical

11. ISLBDEWRE =11. _____
    Confuses or befuddles

12. GIAATBN =12. _____
    Lessening

13. ABSNVADOG =13. _____
    People without a permanent home who move from place to place

14. IVILUCOSY =14. _____
    Aggressively; savagely

15. ODNOISLTEA =15. _____
    Barrenness; dreariness; hopelessness

Cry Beloved Vocabulary Juggle Letters 2 Answer Key

1. OEYVCN = 1. CONVEY
   To communicate or make known

2. OYRLR = 2. LORRY
   A motor truck

3. TRARTIEI = 3. IRRITATE
   Annoy; bother

4. SRPAON = 4. PARSON
   A member of the clergy, especially a Protestant minister

5. STEUIEORRL = 5. IRRESOLUTE
   Unsure of how to act or proceed; undecided

6. TISTACNONR = 6. CONSTRAINT
   Awkwardness

7. IVEEERR = 7. REVERIE
   Daydream

8. EEDPXELPR = 8. PERPLEXED
   Confused or troubled with uncertainty or doubt

9. PAITIOOLTXEN = 9. EXPLOITATION
   Taking advantage of people or a situation for monetary gain

10. CUIRBITOPRNLE = 10. INCORRUPTIBLE
    Incapable of being swayed to do anything immoral, illegal, or unethical

11. ISLBDEWRE = 11. BEWILDERS
    Confuses or befuddles

12. GIAATBN = 12. ABATING
    Lessening

13. ABSNVADOG = 13. VAGABONDS
    People without a permanent home who move from place to place

14. IVILUCOSY = 14. VICIOUSLY
    Aggressively; savagely

15. ODNOISLTEA = 15. DESOLATION
    Barrenness; dreariness; hopelessness

Cry Beloved Vocabulary Juggle Letters 3

1. MNMUOS = 1. _____
   Gather together

2. AUCBEPLL = 2. _____
   Deserving of blame or censure as being wrong

3. SLNEODUI = 3. _____
   A false belief or opinion

4. STPARIOANI = 4. _____
   A strong desire for high achievement; ambition

5. DONSHTAEÏS = 5. _____
   To fill with sudden wonder or amazement

6. RTIRUOLSEE = 6. _____
   Unsure of how to act or proceed; undecided

7. LEACNOGIN = 7. _____
   Suited to one's needs or nature; agreeable

8. SNAOODITLE = 8. _____
   Barrenness; dreariness; hopelessness

9. ELTAVILAC = 9. _____
   To swing indecisively from one course of action or opinion to another

10. LNPRSAYILOIVO =10. _____
    Temporarily

11. ERIELPNGOH =11. _____
    One friendly to Negros and their interests

12. SEITR =12. _____
    One of a series of rows placed one above another

13. LLUNSLEY =13. _____
    Showing a brooding ill humor

14. ODUML =14. _____
    General shape or form

15. DEBIA =15. _____
    To remain in place

Cry Beloved Vocabulary Juggle Letters 3 Answer Key

1. MNMUOS = 1. SUMMON
Gather together

2. AUCBEPLL = 2. CULPABLE
Deserving of blame or censure as being wrong

3. SLNEODUI = 3. DELUSION
A false belief or opinion

4. STPARIOANI = 4. ASPIRATION
A strong desire for high achievement; ambition

5. DONSHTAEIS = 5. ASTONISHED
To fill with sudden wonder or amazement

6. RTIRUOLSEE = 6. IRRESOLUTE
Unsure of how to act or proceed; undecided

7. LEACNOGIN = 7. CONGENIAL
Suited to one's needs or nature; agreeable

8. SNAOODITLE = 8. DESOLATION
Barrenness; dreariness; hopelessness

9. ELTAVILAC = 9. VACILLATE
To swing indecisively from one course of action or opinion to another

10. LNPRSAYILOIVO = 10. PROVISIONALLY
Temporarily

11. ERIELPNGOH = 11. NEGROPHILE
One friendly to Negros and their interests

12. SEITR = 12. TIERS
One of a series of rows placed one above another

13. LLUNSLEY = 13. SULLENLY
Showing a brooding ill humor

14. ODUML = 14. MOULD
General shape or form

15. DEBIA = 15. ABIDE
To remain in place

Cry Beloved Vocabulary Juggle Letters 4

1. OSTTIRCANN   = 1. _____
                        Awkwardness

2. NTEPSOIOIX   = 2. _____
                        A statement or rhetorical discourse intended to give
                        information about or explain difficult material

3. ITAGNAB   = 3. _____
                        Lessening

4. OIESURELRT   = 4. _____
                        Unsure of how to act or proceed; undecided

5. UEYLLSNL   = 5. _____
                        Showing a brooding ill humor

6. SIERDBLWE   = 6. _____
                        Confuses or befuddles

7. SUMONM   = 7. _____
                        Gather together

8. OGRHLEEPNI   = 8. _____
                        One friendly to Negros and their interests

9. DIHNNRCEA   = 9. _____
                        An impediment; something that gets in the way

10. IPLSEEMIRSB   =10. _____
                        Permitted; allowable

11. LRAVATI   =11. _____
                        Work; painful effort; toil

12. YIMMUSOPS   =12. _____
                        A meeting or conference for discussion of a topic

13. ITARRETI   =13. _____
                        Annoy; bother

14. ELLD   =14. _____
                        A small, secluded, wooded valley

15. BNGOGILI   =15. _____
                        Willing to do a service or favor for

Cry Beloved Vocabulary Juggle Letters 4 Answer Key

1. OSTTIRCANN = 1. CONSTRAINT
   Awkwardness

2. NTEPSOIOIX = 2. EXPOSITION
   A statement or rhetorical discourse intended to give information about or explain difficult material

3. ITAGNAB = 3. ABATING
   Lessening

4. OIESURELRT = 4. IRRESOLUTE
   Unsure of how to act or proceed; undecided

5. UEYLLSNL = 5. SULLENLY
   Showing a brooding ill humor

6. SIERDBLWE = 6. BEWILDERS
   Confuses or befuddles

7. SUMONM = 7. SUMMON
   Gather together

8. OGRHLEEPNI = 8. NEGROPHILE
   One friendly to Negros and their interests

9. DIHNNRCEA = 9. HINDRANCE
   An impediment; something that gets in the way

10. IPLSEEMIRSB = 10. PERMISSIBLE
    Permitted; allowable

11. LRAVATI = 11. TRAVAIL
    Work; painful effort; toil

12. YIMMUSOPS = 12. SYMPOSIUM
    A meeting or conference for discussion of a topic

13. ITARRETI = 13. IRRITATE
    Annoy; bother

14. ELLD = 14. DELL
    A small, secluded, wooded valley

15. BNGOGILI = 15. OBLIGING
    Willing to do a service or favor for

ABATING	Lessening
ABIDE	To remain in place
ACCOMPLICES	Those who aid a lawbreaker in a criminal act
AMENDED	Improved
ARRAY	Display
ASPIRATION	A strong desire for high achievement; ambition

ASTONISHED	To fill with sudden wonder or amazement
ASTRAY	Away from the correct path or direction
BEREAVEMENT	Grief over someone's death
BEWILDERS	Confuses or befuddles
BOYCOTT	To abstain from using, buying, or dealing with as a form of protest
BRACKEN	A widespread, often weedy fern

CLEAVE	To split with a sharp instrument
COMPELLED	Forced to action
CONGENIAL	Suited to one's needs or nature; agreeable
CONSTRAINT	Awkwardness
CONVEY	To communicate or make known
CORRUPTED	Marked by immorality and perversion

CULPABLE	Deserving of blame or censure as being wrong
CUNNING	Subtle; deceitful
DELL	A small, secluded, wooded valley
DELUSION	A false belief or opinion
DESOLATION	Barrenness; dreariness; hopelessness
DOGGEDLY	Stubbornly persevering; tenaciously

DUBIOUS	Doubtful
ENRAPT	To fill with rapture or delight
EXPLOITATION	Taking advantage of people or a situation for monetary gain
EXPOSITION	A statement or rhetorical discourse intended to give information about or explain difficult material
FIDELITY	Faithfulness to obligations, or duties
GRATIFY	To please or satisfy

HINDRANCE	An impediment; something that gets in the way
INCORRUPTIBLE	Incapable of being swayed to do anything immoral, illegal, or unethical
INELUCTABLE	Not to be avoided or escaped; inevitable
INEVITABLE	Impossible to avoid or prevent
IRRESOLUTE	Unsure of how to act or proceed; undecided
IRRITATE	Annoy; bother

KLOOF	Ravine
KRAAL	A rural village
LINGO	Language
LORRY	A motor truck
MENACE	A possible danger; a threat
MOULD	General shape or form

MUNICIPALITY	A political unit, such as a city or town, incorporated for local self-government
NEGROPHILE	One friendly to Negros and their interests
OBLIGING	Willing to do a service or favor for
OBSCURE	Hidden; not clearly understood
PARSON	A member of the clergy, especially a Protestant minister
PERMISSIBLE	Permitted; allowable

PERPLEXED	Confused or troubled with uncertainty or doubt
PILGRIMAGE	A long journey or search
PRELUDE	Introduction
PROVISIONALLY	Temporarily
REPENT	To feel such regret for past conduct as to change one's mind regarding it
REPROACHFULLY	Expressing blame

REVERIE	Daydream
SELF-DENUNCIATION	Self-accusation; self-condemnation
SOMBRE	Dark; gloomy; serious; grave
SUBSIDIES	Monetary assistance granted by a government
SULLENLY	Showing a brooding ill humor
SUMMON	Gather together

SYMPOSIUM	A meeting or conference for discussion of a topic
TIERS	One of a series of rows placed one above another
TRAVAIL	Work; painful effort; toil
TREMULOUS	Marked by trembling, quivering, or shaking
UNENDURABLE	Unbearable
VACILLATE	To swing indecisively from one course of action or opinion to another

VAGABONDS	People without a permanent home who move from place to place
VERANDAHS	A porch or balcony, usually roofed, often partly enclosed, extending along the outside of a building
VICIOUSLY	Aggressively; savagely
WARDER	A guard

Cry Beloved Vocabulary

CONSTRAINT	MENACE	REPENT	PERPLEXED	BRACKEN
SELF-DENUNCIATION	INEVITABLE	CLEAVE	COMPELLED	CORRUPTED
UNENDURABLE	ACCOMPLICES	FREE SPACE	ARRAY	INCORRUPTIBLE
EXPLOITATION	TREMULOUS	ASTRAY	REPROACHFULLY	INELUCTABLE
SUBSIDIES	PERMISSIBLE	PROVISIONALLY	CONGENIAL	WARDER

Cry Beloved Vocabulary

BEREAVEMENT	SULLENLY	REVERIE	BEWILDERS	ASTONISHED
SYMPOSIUM	NEGROPHILE	HINDRANCE	TRAVAIL	VICIOUSLY
TIERS	FIDELITY	FREE SPACE	LORRY	VACILLATE
SUMMON	KLOOF	OBLIGING	DOGGEDLY	SOMBRE
IRRESOLUTE	DUBIOUS	ABIDE	MOULD	MUNICIPALITY

Cry Beloved Vocabulary

UNENDURABLE	DELL	SOMBRE	SUBSIDIES	AMENDED
ASTONISHED	ABATING	PRELUDE	CORRUPTED	CULPABLE
PERMISSIBLE	INEVITABLE	FREE SPACE	LORRY	ACCOMPLICES
PARSON	EXPOSITION	LINGO	PROVISIONALLY	DELUSION
MENACE	INELUCTABLE	FIDELITY	REVERIE	DOGGEDLY

Cry Beloved Vocabulary

ARRAY	BEWILDERS	VACILLATE	ABIDE	PILGRIMAGE
IRRITATE	MUNICIPALITY	IRRESOLUTE	HINDRANCE	CONGENIAL
ASPIRATION	INCORRUPTIBLE	FREE SPACE	NEGROPHILE	VAGABONDS
KLOOF	WARDER	BOYCOTT	TREMULOUS	CLEAVE
REPENT	CONSTRAINT	GRATIFY	CUNNING	DESOLATION

Cry Beloved Vocabulary

DOGGEDLY	GRATIFY	FIDELITY	SELF-DENUNCIATION	INEVITABLE
ASTRAY	REVERIE	BEWILDERS	MENACE	SYMPOSIUM
BRACKEN	EXPLOITATION	FREE SPACE	ENRAPT	TRAVAIL
REPENT	ABIDE	KLOOF	AMENDED	BEREAVEMENT
INCORRUPTIBLE	ACCOMPLICES	KRAAL	MUNICIPALITY	PERPLEXED

Cry Beloved Vocabulary

MOULD	ARRAY	WARDER	VERANDAHS	CUNNING
INELUCTABLE	OBLIGING	ASPIRATION	CORRUPTED	DELL
SUBSIDIES	CONGENIAL	FREE SPACE	UNENDURABLE	VAGABONDS
SUMMON	PERMISSIBLE	IRRITATE	CONSTRAINT	VICIOUSLY
DELUSION	SOMBRE	PROVISIONALLY	IRRESOLUTE	VACILLATE

Cry Beloved Vocabulary

VICIOUSLY	REPENT	PILGRIMAGE	CONVEY	TIERS
LORRY	PRELUDE	INCORRUPTIBLE	NEGROPHILE	VACILLATE
OBSCURE	KRAAL	FREE SPACE	SYMPOSIUM	BEWILDERS
OBLIGING	COMPELLED	PROVISIONALLY	ABIDE	ARRAY
CULPABLE	DELUSION	EXPOSITION	CUNNING	DOGGEDLY

Cry Beloved Vocabulary

PERMISSIBLE	ASPIRATION	SELF-DENUNCIATION	REPROACHFULLY	VAGABONDS
ASTONISHED	IRRITATE	EXPLOITATION	CLEAVE	SUMMON
PERPLEXED	CONGENIAL	FREE SPACE	DUBIOUS	TRAVAIL
BEREAVEMENT	LINGO	MOULD	REVERIE	GRATIFY
DELL	AMENDED	BOYCOTT	WARDER	HINDRANCE

Cry Beloved Vocabulary

VACILLATE	PARSON	ENRAPT	BEWILDERS	BRACKEN
ASPIRATION	LINGO	SUBSIDIES	MENACE	CULPABLE
ARRAY	EXPLOITATION	FREE SPACE	REVERIE	INELUCTABLE
KLOOF	AMENDED	NEGROPHILE	OBSCURE	COMPELLED
PERPLEXED	VAGABONDS	ACCOMPLICES	CORRUPTED	REPENT

Cry Beloved Vocabulary

LORRY	SOMBRE	VICIOUSLY	CONVEY	WARDER
IRRESOLUTE	BOYCOTT	PILGRIMAGE	CONGENIAL	DESOLATION
DELUSION	VERANDAHS	FREE SPACE	TREMULOUS	OBLIGING
KRAAL	CLEAVE	GRATIFY	PROVISIONALLY	UNENDURABLE
CONSTRAINT	SYMPOSIUM	ASTONISHED	PRELUDE	TRAVAIL

Cry Beloved Vocabulary

KLOOF	DELUSION	PRELUDE	CULPABLE	TIERS
PARSON	MENACE	BEWILDERS	AMENDED	DESOLATION
ASTONISHED	FIDELITY	FREE SPACE	CONVEY	TRAVAIL
HINDRANCE	ASPIRATION	PERMISSIBLE	VICIOUSLY	SYMPOSIUM
DELL	BEREAVEMENT	REPROACHFULLY	REPENT	WARDER

Cry Beloved Vocabulary

VACILLATE	EXPLOITATION	REVERIE	UNENDURABLE	OBSCURE
SUMMON	BRACKEN	MOULD	INEVITABLE	INCORRUPTIBLE
VERANDAHS	DUBIOUS	FREE SPACE	ASTRAY	ACCOMPLICES
OBLIGING	NEGROPHILE	KRAAL	PILGRIMAGE	CONSTRAINT
ARRAY	LINGO	SUBSIDIES	INELUCTABLE	SULLENLY

Cry Beloved Vocabulary

AMENDED	UNENDURABLE	SOMBRE	OBLIGING	DELL
CONGENIAL	VERANDAHS	IRRITATE	LINGO	PILGRIMAGE
WARDER	SELF-DENUNCIATION	FREE SPACE	EXPLOITATION	FIDELITY
OBSCURE	DESOLATION	INCORRUPTIBLE	VICIOUSLY	PERPLEXED
GRATIFY	EXPOSITION	MUNICIPALITY	ABIDE	SULLENLY

Cry Beloved Vocabulary

DELUSION	CUNNING	LORRY	DOGGEDLY	HINDRANCE
CONSTRAINT	PRELUDE	NEGROPHILE	DUBIOUS	COMPELLED
ABATING	TIERS	FREE SPACE	CONVEY	KRAAL
VAGABONDS	ASTONISHED	SUMMON	BEWILDERS	ASPIRATION
CULPABLE	REPROACHFULLY	CLEAVE	ASTRAY	INELUCTABLE

Cry Beloved Vocabulary

SULLENLY	PERPLEXED	CONVEY	IRRESOLUTE	IRRITATE
LORRY	PROVISIONALLY	REVERIE	SUMMON	MOULD
VACILLATE	TRAVAIL	FREE SPACE	BEWILDERS	ENRAPT
OBSCURE	CONSTRAINT	OBLIGING	KLOOF	SYMPOSIUM
WARDER	PERMISSIBLE	INCORRUPTIBLE	BRACKEN	PARSON

Cry Beloved Vocabulary

ASPIRATION	CUNNING	ACCOMPLICES	PILGRIMAGE	ABATING
DUBIOUS	SUBSIDIES	DELUSION	MENACE	CLEAVE
ASTRAY	INELUCTABLE	FREE SPACE	BEREAVEMENT	DOGGEDLY
GRATIFY	REPENT	KRAAL	VERANDAHS	PRELUDE
ABIDE	AMENDED	TREMULOUS	EXPLOITATION	REPROACHFULLY

Cry Beloved Vocabulary

PILGRIMAGE	VACILLATE	PERPLEXED	MENACE	CONVEY
PARSON	REVERIE	SYMPOSIUM	DELUSION	PERMISSIBLE
CUNNING	SELF-DENUNCIATION	FREE SPACE	DESOLATION	CULPABLE
ARRAY	LORRY	MUNICIPALITY	BOYCOTT	ASPIRATION
BEWILDERS	SOMBRE	SUMMON	ACCOMPLICES	CORRUPTED

Cry Beloved Vocabulary

CONSTRAINT	EXPOSITION	LINGO	BEREAVEMENT	KLOOF
REPENT	REPROACHFULLY	DUBIOUS	MOULD	EXPLOITATION
OBLIGING	PROVISIONALLY	FREE SPACE	VAGABONDS	TIERS
WARDER	DOGGEDLY	TREMULOUS	BRACKEN	DELL
GRATIFY	SUBSIDIES	CONGENIAL	IRRITATE	IRRESOLUTE

Cry Beloved Vocabulary

SELF-DEN UNCIATION	TIERS	AMENDED	ABATING	ASPIRATION
BEWILDERS	DESOLATION	BOYCOTT	VICIOUSLY	ABIDE
UNENDURABLE	REVERIE	FREE SPACE	HINDRANCE	KRAAL
ACCOMPLICES	PERMISSIBLE	DUBIOUS	CONGENIAL	BRACKEN
CONVEY	OBLIGING	DELL	EXPOSITION	PERPLEXED

Cry Beloved Vocabulary

MUNICIPALITY	VERANDAHS	GRATIFY	IRRESOLUTE	PRELUDE
INCORRUPTIBLE	MENACE	SOMBRE	IRRITATE	NEGROPHILE
INEVITABLE	CULPABLE	FREE SPACE	ENRAPT	ARRAY
EXPLOITATION	VACILLATE	PARSON	ASTONISHED	VAGABONDS
SUBSIDIES	INELUCTABLE	FIDELITY	DOGGEDLY	SUMMON

Cry Beloved Vocabulary

REPROACHFULLY	MOULD	IRRESOLUTE	COMPELLED	FIDELITY
PARSON	BOYCOTT	SUBSIDIES	ENRAPT	TRAVAIL
PILGRIMAGE	VICIOUSLY	FREE SPACE	BEREAVEMENT	PRELUDE
ASPIRATION	DOGGEDLY	PERMISSIBLE	SYMPOSIUM	VACILLATE
HINDRANCE	ABIDE	BEWILDERS	GRATIFY	EXPLOITATION

Cry Beloved Vocabulary

INELUCTABLE	INCORRUPTIBLE	CUNNING	REVERIE	ARRAY
MUNICIPALITY	DELUSION	PERPLEXED	CONSTRAINT	CONGENIAL
REPENT	VAGABONDS	FREE SPACE	AMENDED	SELF-DENUNCIATION
ABATING	SOMBRE	CLEAVE	IRRITATE	KLOOF
EXPOSITION	BRACKEN	MENACE	ACCOMPLICES	ASTONISHED

Cry Beloved Vocabulary

UNENDURABLE	ABATING	AMENDED	CONVEY	OBSCURE
PARSON	COMPELLED	SYMPOSIUM	INEVITABLE	DUBIOUS
SUMMON	GRATIFY	FREE SPACE	CONSTRAINT	ARRAY
MOULD	BEWILDERS	DESOLATION	ASPIRATION	ASTONISHED
REVERIE	EXPLOITATION	DELUSION	LINGO	PROVISIONALLY

Cry Beloved Vocabulary

VAGABONDS	DOGGEDLY	TRAVAIL	EXPOSITION	ASTRAY
NEGROPHILE	PERPLEXED	INCORRUPTIBLE	SUBSIDIES	DELL
MUNICIPALITY	PILGRIMAGE	FREE SPACE	CORRUPTED	KLOOF
CUNNING	ACCOMPLICES	CULPABLE	PRELUDE	REPENT
OBLIGING	IRRESOLUTE	SELF-DENUNCIATION	PERMISSIBLE	TIERS

Cry Beloved Vocabulary

TIERS	ABATING	PROVISIONALLY	KRAAL	GRATIFY
COMPELLED	IRRESOLUTE	TRAVAIL	CORRUPTED	NEGROPHILE
BEREAVEMENT	CULPABLE	FREE SPACE	REVERIE	CONGENIAL
OBSCURE	VERANDAHS	INCORRUPTIBLE	MUNICIPALITY	OBLIGING
KLOOF	DELL	DELUSION	VICIOUSLY	ARRAY

Cry Beloved Vocabulary

BEWILDERS	CONSTRAINT	WARDER	BOYCOTT	PARSON
SOMBRE	ABIDE	DUBIOUS	UNENDURABLE	AMENDED
SUBSIDIES	PRELUDE	FREE SPACE	IRRITATE	REPENT
DOGGEDLY	VACILLATE	ACCOMPLICES	PERMISSIBLE	CUNNING
FIDELITY	CLEAVE	ASPIRATION	MOULD	EXPLOITATION

Cry Beloved Vocabulary

BRACKEN	OBSCURE	BEWILDERS	HINDRANCE	IRRESOLUTE
TRAVAIL	KLOOF	PERPLEXED	TREMULOUS	DELUSION
VICIOUSLY	PARSON	FREE SPACE	DESOLATION	FIDELITY
REVERIE	AMENDED	INCORRUPTIBLE	CULPABLE	DUBIOUS
SYMPOSIUM	KRAAL	PRELUDE	IRRITATE	NEGROPHILE

Cry Beloved Vocabulary

ARRAY	VAGABONDS	ACCOMPLICES	ASTONISHED	OBLIGING
PILGRIMAGE	DOGGEDLY	CONSTRAINT	PERMISSIBLE	INELUCTABLE
CONGENIAL	VERANDAHS	FREE SPACE	GRATIFY	SUMMON
UNENDURABLE	EXPOSITION	CLEAVE	EXPLOITATION	BEREAVEMENT
REPROACHFULLY	MUNICIPALITY	VACILLATE	ABIDE	ENRAPT

Cry Beloved Vocabulary

CORRUPTED	REPROACHFULLY	SUMMON	CUNNING	ENRAPT
UNENDURABLE	MENACE	ACCOMPLICES	KRAAL	EXPOSITION
OBSCURE	DELL	FREE SPACE	COMPELLED	PARSON
LINGO	PERPLEXED	SELF-DENUNCIATION	TREMULOUS	DUBIOUS
PILGRIMAGE	SULLENLY	DOGGEDLY	ABATING	VAGABONDS

Cry Beloved Vocabulary

DELUSION	WARDER	BEWILDERS	VACILLATE	VICIOUSLY
ABIDE	MOULD	REPENT	NEGROPHILE	TIERS
OBLIGING	EXPLOITATION	FREE SPACE	ARRAY	KLOOF
ASPIRATION	SOMBRE	CULPABLE	CONSTRAINT	IRRITATE
INCORRUPTIBLE	ASTRAY	CONVEY	REVERIE	IRRESOLUTE

Cry Beloved Vocabulary

CONSTRAINT	SOMBRE	NEGROPHILE	SUBSIDIES	GRATIFY
COMPELLED	TIERS	OBSCURE	CUNNING	HINDRANCE
LINGO	INELUCTABLE	FREE SPACE	EXPLOITATION	ASPIRATION
CONGENIAL	BOYCOTT	KLOOF	CLEAVE	LORRY
MENACE	FIDELITY	INCORRUPTIBLE	OBLIGING	IRRITATE

Cry Beloved Vocabulary

EXPOSITION	PILGRIMAGE	PERPLEXED	PARSON	IRRESOLUTE
ENRAPT	CORRUPTED	PERMISSIBLE	VAGABONDS	DELUSION
VACILLATE	VICIOUSLY	FREE SPACE	DUBIOUS	TREMULOUS
REPENT	DESOLATION	KRAAL	WARDER	CULPABLE
BRACKEN	CONVEY	ASTRAY	PROVISIONALLY	VERANDAHS

www.ingramcontent.com/pod-product-compliance
Lightning Source LLC
Chambersburg PA
CBHW081453070526
44586CB00019B/2338